green

green

modern vegetarian recipes

flip shelton

Hardie Grant Books

My mother – for developing my appetite

My father – for making me an animal lover

My boyfriend – for being a fabulous eating companion

Published in 2002
by Hardie Grant Books
12 Claremont Street
South Yarra, Victoria 3141, Australia
www.hardiegrant.com.au

National Library of Australia Cataloguing-in-Publication Data:

Shelton, Flip, 1966– .
    Green: modern vegetarian recipes.
    Includes index.
    ISBN 1 74064 052 7.
    1. Vegetarian cookery. I. Title.
641.5636

Cover and text design by text-art
Photography by Greg Elms
Styling by Virginia Dowzer
Typeset by text-art
Printed and bound by Tien Wah Press, Singapore

The Publishers are grateful to Dinosaur Designs for their generous assistance and for the loan of props.

Contents

Introduction

Good recipe books are like travel guides – they should be tempting, interesting, sometimes adventurous, sometimes familiar, but they should always provide satisfaction and contentment. *Green* is a collection of recipes to help you survive the daily grind of getting good food into your gob quickly, easily and relatively cheaply, while also giving you some food for thought.

I'm no chef. My mother, necessity and mistakes have been my teachers. As a person on the go, I look for interesting dishes that can be thrown together simply and often quickly. I train with a triathlon squad six to twelve times a week, which means I am always hungry and I need food to fuel me through sessions and help me recover afterwards. I quite literally eat on the run – or bike! My cycling jersey acts as a pantry for food that can be eaten with one hand; and my running shorts are often stuffed with goodies for a long run. I completed my first Ironman competition (3.8-kilometre swim, 180.2-kilometre bike ride, 42.2-kilometre run) this year, and am looking forward to the next one.

My big beef – if you'll pardon the expression – with many vegetarian cookbooks is their reliance on dairy products, wheat flour, eggs and bread. While these ingredients do appear in *Green*, they play a small role. I prefer to concentrate on organic, seasonal produce and ingredients that have undergone as little processing as possible.

There are no complicated techniques and no fancy-schmancy tricks, other than a few shortcuts or tips. Some dishes do take a while to cook, but they don't need constant vigilance or the latest high-tech equipment (although a blender and a juicer do come in handy from time to time).

You'll see that many of these recipes serve just one or two people. Most of us live in smaller households these days. My serves are generous, so a recipe for two may provide a little something for lunch the next day. If there are four mouths to feed at your place, just double the quantities.

The measurements are here only as a guide. It was only when I started compiling this book that I bought a set of scales and measuring cups, so you'll often find me using handfuls of herbs, or sprinklings of spices, rather than exact measures. If you don't have or don't like a certain ingredient, swap it for something else. Make it your dish.

I want *Green* to show that vegetarian food can be sexy, exciting and not just a phase. I want to show you that recipes don't need to be complicated to be tasty or, dare I say it, good for you. I want you to say, 'I can do that', and perhaps discover some new ingredients along the way. But mostly I want to encourage you to have fun in the kitchen.

Thanks to Amanda Finnis for finding me at 3RRR and believing my recipes were worth publishing, and thanks to all those family and friends who ate and tested the food.

Happy eating.

I truly believe the saying 'Eat breakfast like a king, lunch like a prince, and dinner like a pauper' – at least, until dinnertime rolls around! I vary my breakfast as much as possible because I reckon the body gets bored with the same start to every day. If you excite your tastebuds every morning, you charge your body with a new energy each day.

Breakfast

Yoghurt Rockmelon Boat

Use your nose to test whether the rockmelon smells sweet and ripe. Then close your eyes and let your tastebuds do the rest.

Serves 1.

½ rockmelon (cantaloupe)

½–1 cup (4–8 fl oz) yoghurt (preferably biodynamic, although Greek-style yoghurt is deliciously rich)

1 cup green grapes

50 g (¼ cup) chopped walnuts

1 teaspoon brown sugar

Scoop the seeds out of the rockmelon and pile the yoghurt into the cavity. Top with grapes and walnuts and sprinkle with brown sugar.

Chill for 5 minutes before serving to allow flavours to infuse.

Stewed Fruit

Raw fruit can be hard on the tummy first thing in the morning, so stewed fruit is a good alternative. It also makes a great snack or dessert. Cook the fruit in water, or spark it up with spices and other flavourings. Seasonal fruit should be sweet enough, but if you like, add apple concentrate, honey, rice syrup or sugar.

Apples: I only ever use Granny Smiths because they hold their shape and I like their tartness. Peel, core and cut apples into 8 wedges. Put into a heavy-based saucepan with enough water to come about halfway up the apples. Add a few whole cloves or a cinnamon stick. Bring to the boil, then simmer, uncovered, over a low heat for 15 minutes. For dessert, sprinkle on slivered almonds and a few sultanas.

Cherries: wash but leave whole. Put into a small heavy-based saucepan and partly cover with water. Bring to the boil, then simmer over a low heat for 10 minutes.

Pears: peel, core and quarter. Put in a medium-sized heavy-based saucepan and barely cover with water. Add either a sprinkling of ground cinnamon, nutmeg or cloves. Bring to the boil, then reduce heat and simmer for 20–25 minutes, or until soft. Serve with yoghurt and chopped pistachios.

Plums: put plums into a large heavy-based saucepan in a single layer. Add enough water to come halfway up the plums (don't submerge them). Toss in some crushed cardamom pods or some star anise. Bring to the boil, then reduce heat and simmer, uncovered, for 15 minutes, or longer if you want them really soft. For dessert, serve with a dollop of yoghurt, some crushed walnuts and a few drops of vanilla extract or seeds from a vanilla bean.

Quinces: peel, core and cut into eighths. Put into a heavy-based saucepan and cover with water. Quinces can be tart, so some brown sugar or honey may be called for. Bring to the boil, then reduce heat and simmer for about 45 minutes, or until soft. Add a little more water if they look dry. The longer and slower you cook quinces, the pinker they become. If you like, add grated fresh ginger towards the end of cooking.

Rhubarb: discard leaves, wash stalks and cut into 5 cm (2 in) lengths. Add enough orange juice to cover the base of the saucepan and bring to the boil over a medium heat. Reduce to low and simmer for 5–10 minutes, or until the rhubarb softens. Towards the end of cooking, stir in 1–2 tablespoons of good balsamic vinegar, 1 tablespoon of rosewater or orange blossom water.

Tomato and Ricotta Toast

A quick, light breakfast or brunch in summer, when tomatoes are at their best.

Serves 1.

2 slices sourdough bread

2 tablespoons ricotta

1 ripe tomato, thinly sliced

2 fresh basil leaves, finely chopped

olive oil

sea salt and cracked black pepper to taste

Toast the bread and spread half the ricotta on each piece. Cover with tomato slices and top with basil leaves. Drizzle with a little olive oil and add salt and pepper to taste.

4

Crumpets

I loved crumpets as a kid. And when I made my own, I loved them even more. To cook them, you'll need metal egg rings or 5 cm (2 inch) metal cookie cutters.

Makes 24.

4 cups plain (all-purpose) flour

2 tablespoons baking powder (baking soda)

a pinch of sea salt

1 teaspoon sugar

7 g (¼ oz, 1 sachet) active dry yeast

3 cups (24 fl oz) lukewarm water

Sift the flour and baking powder together into a large mixing bowl. Stir in salt and sugar.

In a separate bowl, combine the yeast and warm water and stir until well combined.

Add yeast and water to flour mixture and beat quickly until just combined, taking care not to over-beat the batter. If you have time, let the batter rest for 30 minutes.

Lightly grease a heavy-based frying pan and heat at a low temperature, or use a non-stick electric frypan set to 120°C/250°F. Grease the egg rings and place them in the pan, then spoon in enough of the batter to almost fill the egg rings. Cook the crumpets gently for 10–12 minutes, or until surface is covered with holes, like honeycomb.

Carefully remove the rings, flip the crumpets over, cover the frying pan and cook for a further 3–5 minutes, until the batter has set but has not browned.

Allow the crumpets to cool, then toast them and top with butter, honey or Banana Jam (see page 6).

Banana Jam

Most jams are loaded with sugar, but using ripe bananas and sultanas means you'll need to add only a little extra sweetness. Replace the cinnamon sticks with a couple of cardamom pods for a different but equally wonderful flavour. If you want a runnier consistency, add a little water during cooking.

Makes about 2 cups.

1 kg (2 lb) ripe bananas, chopped

½ cup (4 fl oz) lemon juice (about 3 lemons)

zest of 1 lemon

½ cup brown sugar

1 cinnamon stick

1 tablespoon shredded coconut

2 tablespoons sultanas (golden raisins)

Place the bananas, lemon juice and zest, sugar and cinnamon stick in a heavy-based saucepan and cook on low, uncovered, for 15–20 minutes, stirring often to prevent the mixture from sticking to the saucepan. Stir in the coconut and sultanas and cook for a further 5 minutes.

Remove the cinnamon stick, taking care not to burn yourself.

Spoon the warm jam into sterilised jars and allow jam to cool before storing in the fridge. As this contains little sugar to act as a preservative, eat within a few days. (That won't be hard!)

Almond Butter

If you are a fan of peanut butter, you'll love this. But be warned: it's addictive. For a change, make it with peanuts, brazil nuts or cashews, or a combo.

Makes 2 small jars.

1 cup raw almonds, blanched or unblanched

2 cups (16 fl oz) water

¼ cup (2 fl oz) light olive oil (or flaxseed, safflower or peanut oil)

¼ cup (2 fl oz) apple concentrate

Cover nuts with water and soak for 48 hours. Drain and put the soaked nuts in the bowl of a food processor. Partially grind nuts, then slowly add the oil and apple concentrate (adding more of each if necessary) until you reach the desired consistency. Store almond butter in the fridge. Tastes best late at night!

Orange Couscous

A colourful way to start the day, this also makes an excellent salad.

Serves 2.

1 cup (8 fl oz) freshly squeezed orange juice (about 3 oranges)

½ cup couscous

5 dried apricots, thinly sliced

a few Chilean Flame raisins

a few flaked almonds

a sprinkling of shredded coconut

a sprinkling of ground cinnamon

a few mint leaves, finely sliced

Heat the orange juice in a medium-sized heavy-based saucepan and bring it almost to the boil. Add the couscous and dried fruits to the saucepan and give a quick stir, then remove the saucepan from the heat, cover, and leave it to stand for 5 minutes.

Return to the stove and cook on very low heat for 2 minutes, stirring constantly with a wooden spoon.

Separate the grains by fluffing with a fork, stir in the almonds, coconut, cinnamon and mint leaves and serve warm.

Facing page: Orange Couscous (recipe this page).

Hotcake Stack

Bigger than a pancake, thinner than a pikelet and twice as delicious as either.

Makes 3 hotcakes.

1 cup self-raising wholemeal flour or 1 cup wholemeal flour and
    2 teaspoons baking powder (baking soda)

1 cup (8 fl oz) soy drink

1 egg, beaten

1 teaspoon vanilla extract

1 tablespoon apple concentrate or honey

a sprinkling of ground cinnamon

a sprinkling of ground nutmeg

1 tablespoon vegetable oil

Sift the flour into a mixing bowl. Make a hollow in the middle and stir in the soy drink and egg. Add the vanilla extract, apple concentrate and spices and stir until well combined. Let the mixture stand for at least 30 minutes to relax the gluten (the elastic component of flour), making the hotcakes lighter.

Warm a little of the oil in a heavy-based frying pan over a medium heat, then spoon in about a ⅓ cup (one large ladleful) of batter. Cook for about 2½ minutes, or until the underside is golden, then flip over to cook the other side until golden, about 1 minute.

Heat a little more oil in the frying pan and repeat the process. Remember that the frying pan will heat up, so reduce the heat to low for the second and third hotcakes to avoid burning them.

When all the mixture has been used, stack hotcakes on a plate and top with whatever takes your fancy.

Suggested toppings: Firm ricotta; mango slices; banana slices; strawberry purée; honey; chopped mint leaves; lemon juice; chopped nuts.

9

Facing page: Hotcake Stack (recipe this page).

Bircher Muesli

Tailor your flavours using any combination of dried and fresh fruit and nuts. If you don't like yoghurt, add more mashed banana and fruit juice. Double the recipe to make enough for several days' breakfasts – it tastes even better after a little time in the fridge.

Serves 1–2.

1 cup rolled oats

½ cup (4 fl oz) apple juice (or freshly squeezed orange juice)

½ cup (4 fl oz) yoghurt

⅛ cup currants

⅛ cup slivered almonds

a sprinkling of ground nutmeg

a sprinkling of ground cinnamon

½ Granny Smith apple, grated (skin on) to serve

½ banana, sliced or mashed to serve

seasonal berries and mint sprigs to serve

Combine the rolled oats, apple juice, yoghurt, currants, almonds, nutmeg and cinnamon in a large bowl and stir together. Chill overnight (or for at least two hours).

To serve, stir in the grated apple and banana, put into a bowl and garnish with seasonal berries and mint sprigs.

Suggested additions or substitutions: Seasonal berries; passionfruit pulp; sultanas (golden raisins) or dried cranberries; roughly chopped dried apricots or dried pears; chopped nuts; pepitas (pumpkin seeds).

Brown Rice Brekkie

There's always a pot of cooked brown rice on the stove at my place – I eat a bowl of this great grain every day. Cook the rice ahead to speed things up in the morning, then warm it briefly in the microwave before serving. This is also good cold.

Serves 2.

1 cup brown rice

2 cups (16 fl oz) water

2 tablespoons LSA

6 peach slices, fresh or canned

¼ cup sultanas (golden raisins)

1 tablespoon yoghurt

Put the rice and water into a medium-sized heavy-based saucepan over a medium heat and bring to the boil. Reduce the heat to low, put a heat diffuser under the saucepan and simmer gently, covered, for 40 minutes. DO NOT lift the lid. Allow the rice to sit for 5 minutes with the lid on before venturing into the pot.

To serve, place a cup of brown rice in each bowl and top with LSA, peach slices, sultanas and yoghurt.

Grainy Porridge

Thick and grainy, perfect for the coldest of winter mornings. Make the basic mixture ahead, then cook it up as you need it (but remember, you'll need to soak the grains overnight). The quantities for the grain mixture are enough for 4.

Serves 1.

Grain Mixture

1 cup rolled oats

¼ cup rice flakes

¼ cup rye flakes

¼ cup barley flakes

¼ cup triticale flakes

½ cup Grainy Porridge mix

1 cup (8 fl oz) water

½ cup (4 fl oz) water (or oat/rice/soy drink)

a sprinkling of ground cinnamon

a sprinkling of ground nutmeg

a few roughly chopped brazil nuts

a few roughly chopped dried apricots

a sprinkling of sesame seeds

honey to taste

soy drink or yoghurt to serve, optional

To make the Grain Mixture, combine the rolled oats, and rice, rye, barley and triticale flakes in an airtight container.

To cook, soak the Grain Porridge mixture overnight in 1 cup (8 fl oz) water.

Next morning, put the grains in a small heavy-based saucepan and add ½ cup (4 fl oz) water or other liquid, cinnamon and nutmeg. Bring to the boil over a medium heat, then reduce heat a little and simmer, stirring often, for about 5 minutes, or until the grains soften.

Remove from the heat and stir in the nuts, apricots, sesame seeds and honey, plus a splash of soy drink or a dollop of yoghurt – whichever you prefer.

Apple Risotto

The perfect breakfast after an early training session, it can also be transformed into a decadent dessert.

Serves 1 starving person after training; 2 people from slumber or 4 people as a dessert.

½ cup arborio or medium-grain white rice

1½ cups (12 fl oz) water (use only 1 cup/8 fl oz for medium-grain white rice)

1 cup (8 fl oz) apple juice

1 Granny Smith apple, peeled and diced, or a handful of dried apple

a sprinkling of ground nutmeg

a sprinkling of ground cinnamon

1 teaspoon brown sugar or 1 tablespoon apple concentrate/honey

1 tablespoon yoghurt

Place the rice, water, apple juice, apple, nutmeg and cinnamon in a medium-sized heavy-based saucepan. Bring to the boil, then reduce the heat to low and cook for 25–30 minutes, or until the rice is soft, stirring frequently to prevent it from sticking to the saucepan. Towards the end of cooking, stir in the brown sugar.

To serve, spoon into a bowl and stir in the yoghurt.

To make as a dessert, replace some of the water with sticky dessert wine and caramelise the chopped apple separately in 1 tablespoon brown sugar, ¼ cup (2 fl oz) water and a nip of brandy. Stir the apple and the seeds of a vanilla bean into the rice towards the end of cooking. Serve with a little cream or yoghurt. Leftovers can be warmed in the microwave or eaten cold.

Scrambled Tofu

While this is a wonderfully substantial breakfast, it also makes a great Sunday night meal in front of the television, accompanied by roasted tomatoes, mushrooms and spinach.

Serves 1.

200 g (7 oz) firm tofu

1 teaspoon ground turmeric

1 small piece fresh ginger, finely grated

1 garlic clove, finely chopped

1 teaspoon chopped coriander (cilantro) leaves

sea salt and cracked black pepper to taste

1 tablespoon vegetable oil

lemon juice to taste

1 slice pumpernickel bread

In a small bowl, mash tofu with a fork or potato masher until it is crumbly. Add the turmeric, ginger, garlic, coriander leaves, salt and pepper and mix well.

Heat the oil in a wok or a large heavy-based frying pan over a medium heat. Add the tofu mixture and cook until the tofu is warmed through.

Remove from the heat. Pile the tofu mixture on to pumpernickel slice, drizzle with a little lemon juice, and serve.

Egg Stack

A great way to wake up your tastebuds. To make it, you'll need a couple of egg rings or large metal cookie cutters.

Serves 1.

2 eggs

sea salt and cracked black pepper to taste

small handful chopped fresh herbs (such as dill, basil, parsley)

handful beansprouts (optional)

sweet chilli sauce to serve

In a small bowl, lightly beat the eggs with a little salt and pepper.

Heat a non-stick frying pan over a medium heat. Grease 2 egg rings and place them in the centre of the pan. Pour half the egg mixture into each ring and cook for 3 minutes, or until the eggs are starting to firm but the tops are still a little soft and runny.

Using a spatula, carefully flip the eggs and cook for another 30 seconds. The mixture may spill a little but don't worry.

Place one egg on a plate, sprinkle with chopped herbs and a few beansprouts, then top with remaining egg. Drizzle with sweet chilli sauce and serve.

Fluffy Choc-omelette

OK, so this is not a super-healthy way to start the day but it does makes an indulgent Sunday brunch.

Serves 1.

2 eggs, separated

1–2 tablespoons ground hazelnuts

olive oil spray

25 g (1 oz) good chocolate, melted

Preheat oven to 220°C/425°F/gas mark 7.

Lightly grease a deep baking dish (about 24 x 14 cm/9 x 5½ inch) with olive oil spray. Add ground hazelnuts and swirl to coat the sides of the dish.

Separate the eggs and in a medium-sized bowl, beat the yolks until thick and pale. Stir in the melted chocolate.

In a small bowl, whisk the egg whites until firm peaks form. Gently fold the whites into the yolk mixture and stir carefully to mix.

Pour the mixture into the prepared baking dish, and bake for 10 minutes. Serve hot.

Buy yourself a birthday present – no matter what the date or month – and make it a juicer. That way, you'll say 'cheers' every day.

The other piece of essential equipment for making these delish drinks is a blender.

Drinks & Juices

Banana Smoothie

Give your digestive system a rest by drinking, rather than eating, your vitamins and minerals. When your bananas start to blacken in the fruit bowl, peel and store them in an airtight plastic bag in the freezer until the next smoothie craving strikes.

Serves 1.

1 ripe banana, chopped

1 cup (8 fl oz) rice/oat/soy drink

1 tablespoon psyllium husks

1 teaspoon sunflower seeds

sprinkling ground nutmeg

honey to taste

Put all the ingredients in a blender and mix well.

Luscious Lecithin Liquid Brekkie

The perfect drink for those days when you have to get up and go. Wheatgrass, which contains loads of essential vitamins and minerals, turns it a fabulous green.

Serves 1.

1 cup (8 fl oz) vanilla soy drink

1 banana or peach

1 teaspoon lecithin

1 teaspoon powdered wheatgrass

Blend all the ingredients until smooth. Drink on the go, from a travel mug.

Lassi

An excellent drink to serve alongside, or after, a spicy curry.

Serves 1.

1 cup (8 fl oz) thick yoghurt

3 strands saffron

50 g (¼ cup) pistachio nuts

¼ teaspoon cardamom

Blend all ingredients together until smooth.

Detox

Spring-clean your system – in summer, autumn, winter or spring.

Serves 1.

1 small beetroot (beet)

1 Granny Smith apple

1 medium-sized carrot

1 celery stalk

100 g (4 oz) pineapple

1 small piece fresh ginger

Put everything into a juicer. Pour into a glass and sip slowly, but watch out for the beetroot moustache!

Orange and Lemonade

Makes about 4 litres (8 pints).

½–1 cup brown sugar

1 litre (2 pints) water

zest and juice of 3 oranges

zest and juice of 3 lemons

soda water, mint leaves and ice to serve

Dissolve the sugar in water and add the orange and lemon zest and juice. Bring to the boil and simmer for a few minutes. Transfer the mixture to a sterilised bottle, allow to cool, then refrigerate.

To serve, add about ¼ cup of the mixture to 1 cup soda water, and add ice and mint.

Sangria

Picture sitting on a deck some sunny Sunday. Now picture a pitcher of this.

Makes 4 litres (8 pints).

1 litre (2 pints) fruity red wine

300 ml (10 fl oz) mineral water

⅓ cup (2½ fl oz) lemon juice

⅓ cup caster (granulated) sugar

1 lemon, sliced

1 orange, sliced

ice to serve

Pour the wine and mineral water into a large serving jug.

Whisk together the lemon juice and sugar in a cup until the sugar has dissolved. Add to the wine and stir again. Add lemon and orange slices. Serve over ice, preferably chilled.

Berry Blitz

A berry bright way to start the day.

Serves 1.

100 g (1 cup) fresh raspberries

100 g (1 cup) fresh strawberries

1 cup (8 fl oz) cranberry juice

Put all the ingredients in a blender and pulse until smooth. Serve immediately.

Pineapple Crush

A golden ray of sunshine in a glass.

Serves 1.

1 cup fresh pineapple pieces

several ice cubes

a splash of lime cordial

4–5 finely chopped fresh mint leaves

Toss all ingredients into a blender and pulse until well combined but not 'watery'.

Allo Aloe

Aloe vera has been described as a natural healer as it contains many essential amino acids, vitamins, minerals, proteins and enzymes. Give yourself a dose whenever you feel low.

Serves 1.

¼ continental cucumber

½ Granny Smith apple

juice of ½ lemon

1 tablespoon aloe vera liquid

Juice the cucumber and apple. Stir in the lemon juice and aloe vera and serve.

Carrot Pep

This has a pretty orange colour, a delicate floral scent and a great texture.

Serves 1.

3 carrots

150 g (5 oz) silken tofu

1 tablespoon almond meal

1 tablespoon rosewater

Juice the carrots then blend with the silken tofu, almond meal and rosewater until smooth.

Facing page: Allo Aloe (recipe this page); Carrot Pep (recipe this page).

Spiced Tea

Spice up a pot of tea by adding 1–2 teaspoons of this blend with the tea leaves. Drink black or white.

Makes enough for 2–4 pots.

1½ teaspoons ground ginger

1 teaspoon ground cardamom

½ teaspoon ground cinnamon

½ teaspoon ground nutmeg

¼ teaspoon ground cloves

¼ teaspoon mace

Combine all ingredients. For a more intense flavour and aroma, put the spices into a small frying pan over a low heat and dry fry them, stirring so they don't burn. Store in a small airtight container.

Spiced Coffee

Wake up and smell the coffee! But it's also a wonderful way to end your day.

Serves 1.

3 teaspoons good ground coffee

2 cinnamon sticks

6 fennel seeds, crushed

1 teaspoon brown sugar

Combine all of the ingredients in a coffee plunger, add boiling water and allow to stand for 5 minutes before pouring.

25

Facing page: Mango and Macadamia Salad (recipe page 29).

Salads are have undergone a radical change, and moved on from the combination of lettuce, tomatoes and cucumber with a white vinegar vinaigrette. These days salads are most certainly not rabbit food, and almost any combination of fresh ingredients can be tossed together with a dressing to create meals with body and style.

Salads

Watermelon and Chive Salad

Take a trip back to the '70s, when this simple, radiant salad was groovy. It still is.

Serves 4.

500 g (1 lb) ripe watermelon

small bunch chives, chopped

Cut the rind off the watermelon and chop the flesh into 2.5 cm (1 in) dice. Put the watermelon into salad bowl. Add the chopped chives and toss gently. Serve cold.

Tomato and Bocconcini Salad

Is it a light salad, an appetiser or a healthy snack? You decide.

Serves 2.

4 ripe tomatoes

4 bocconcini balls

5 fresh basil leaves, chopped

extra-virgin olive oil

sea salt and cracked black pepper to taste

Cut tomatoes and bocconcini into slices of the same thickness.

Arrange them on a plate (or slices of bread or crackers), alternating between a slice of tomato, a little basil and a bocconcini slice. Drizzle with olive oil and season to taste with salt and pepper.

Mango and Macadamia Salad

I can't believe that Eve was tempted by an apple – surely it was a mango, that most sensual and indulgent of fruits. The only other way to eat a mango is alone and on its own.

Serves 1 serious mango lover.

200 g (7 oz) soba (buckwheat) noodles

1 large ripe mango

handful rocket (arugula) leaves

50 g (¼ cup) roughly chopped macadamia nuts or peanuts

Lime Dressing

juice of 1 lime

2 tablespoons rice vinegar

¼ teaspoon chilli powder or to taste

1 teaspoon brown sugar

Break the noodles in half and boil them in a large pot of water for 7 minutes, or until they are tender but still firm. Drain and refresh under cold running water. Drain again.

Cut the two cheeks of the mango from the pip and slip a large dessertspoon between the skin and flesh. Following the line of the skin, gently carve out the flesh, so that it sits on the spoon perfectly. Cut the mango into slices.

To make the Lime Dressing, combine the lime juice, vinegar, chilli powder and sugar in a small bowl and mix well.

Toss the noodles, mango slices, rocket, nuts into a serving bowl, drizzle on the dressing and stir gently.

Waldorf Salad

This crunchy autumn salad is also delicious with raspberry vinegar instead of the apple dressing.

Serves 2.

1 Granny Smith apple, peel on

1 celery stalk

1 cup green grapes

100 g (½ cup) roughly chopped walnut pieces

50 g (2 oz) feta, diced or crumbled (or bocconcini or blue cheese)

Apple Dressing

¼ cup (2 fl oz) lemon juice (about 2 lemons)

1 tablespoon apple concentrate

a sprinkling of ground cinnamon

a sprinkling of ground nutmeg

Cut the apple into quarters, remove the core and slice finely. Cut the celery into thin crescents. Toss into a medium-sized bowl with the grapes, walnuts and feta. Drizzle with dressing and serve.

To make the Apple Dressing, put the lemon juice, apple concentrate and spices into a small bowl and mix well.

Green Pear and Blue Cheese Salad

Research shows that men prefer soft pears and women prefer firm ones. It's certainly true at my house. For this salad, you can take your pick. But remember: pears ripen from the centre, so don't leave them too long in the fruit bowl.

Serves 2.

1 ripe green pear, such as William

handful rocket (arugula) leaves (or baby spinach leaves mixed with watercress)

50 g (2 oz) blue cheese, crumbled

50 g (¼ cup) raw or toasted walnut pieces

a drizzle of lemon juice

a drizzle of balsamic vinegar

a drizzle of olive oil

sea salt and cracked black pepper to taste

Cut the pears in half, remove the core and cut into 8 wedges.

Make a bed of rocket on a plate. Pile on the pear and walnut pieces and sprinkle with crumbled cheese. Drizzle with lemon juice, balsamic vinegar and olive oil. Season to taste with salt and pepper.

Terrific Tabbouleh Salad

Cracked wheat has been used in Middle Eastern cookery for the past 4000 years, which makes me a relative newcomer to it! This tangy Lebanese salad makes a great filling for pita pockets and sandwiches.

Serves 4.

1 cup cracked wheat

2 cups (16 fl oz) cold water

4 tomatoes

2 spring onions (scallions), whole, finely chopped

2 cups chopped mint leaves

1 cup chopped flat-leaf parsley

1 tablespoon olive oil

juice and zest of 1 lemon

sea salt and cracked black pepper to taste

Soak the cracked wheat in the cold water for 1 hour. Drain. Place a clean, dry tea towel on a wire rack or baking tray, leaving enough overhanging to fold back over. Spread the cracked wheat over the tea towel and cover with the overhanging cloth. Gently press the towel to absorb excess water, then allow to stand for 15 minutes.

Meanwhile, cut each tomato into 8 wedges and remove the seeds.

In a large bowl, combine the cracked wheat, tomatoes, spring onions, parsley and mint.

In a small bowl, mix together the olive oil and lemon juice and rind. Season to taste with salt and pepper. Drizzle over the salad, mix well and serve immediately.

Zorba's Salad

This is one of those freewheeling dishes where you can just toss together the ingredients in a bowl, with no measuring and no mixing. The quantities here are a guide only.

Serves 2.

4 ripe tomatoes, roughly chopped

½ long cucumber, roughly chopped

100 g (4 oz) feta cheese, diced or crumbled

100 g (½ cup) kalamata olives, pitted and halved

a handful of parsley, roughly chopped

juice of 1 lemon

a drizzle of olive oil

a drizzle of balsamic vinegar

sea salt and cracked black pepper to taste

Toss the tomatoes, cucumber, feta, olives and parsley into a medium-sized serving bowl. Pour on the lemon juice and a good freehand drizzle of oil and vinegar. Season to taste with salt and pepper and serve.

Sort-of Caesar Salad

The best aspects of Caesar and niçoise salads go into this meal-in-a-bowl.

Serves 2.

200 g (7 oz) waxy potato, skin on, diced

100 g (3½ oz) green beans, trimmed and cut in half

1 egg

1 small cos (romaine) lettuce

50 g (1½ oz) marinated olives, cut into quarters

100 g (3½ oz) cherry tomatoes, halved

Sort-of Caesar Dressing

2 tablespoons olive oil

3 tablespoons balsamic vinegar

1 teaspoon mustard

sea salt and cracked black pepper to taste

Steam the potato and beans in a vegetable steamer over rapidly boiling water until tender, 10–15 minutes. Allow to cool.

Cover the egg with cold water in a small saucepan and bring to the boil over a medium heat. Boil for 8 minutes, then drain and immediately cover the egg with cold water to stop it cooking. Allow to cool before peeling and slicing.

Separate the lettuce leaves and wash well. Tear into bite-sized pieces and toss into a medium-sized bowl. Add the potato, beans, egg slices, olives and tomatoes. Drizzle with dressing.

To make the Sort-of Caesar Dressing, put the oil, vinegar and mustard into a small bowl and whisk until the mixture thickens. Season to taste with salt and pepper.

Kohlrabi Slaw

You may have tried coleslaw. Well, wait until you try kohlrabi slaw, a winter salad with a warming mustard dressing. Finely sliced fennel or chopped yellow capsicum are other fab additions.

Serves 4.

½ cup peeled and grated purple kohlrabi

½ cup peeled and grated celeriac

2 carrots, peeled and grated

¼ cabbage, core removed and shredded

¼ cup sultanas (golden raisins)

handful alfalfa sprouts

Mustard Dressing

1 egg yolk

1 teaspoon prepared mustard, or to taste

1 tablespoon white wine vinegar

3 tablespoons light olive oil

Mix together the kohlrabi, celeriac, carrot, cabbage, sultanas and alfalfa in a salad bowl.

To make the Mustard Dressing, place the egg yolk, mustard and vinegar in a small bowl and whisk (or blend in a small food processor) until well combined. Slowly pour in the oil, while continuing to beat, until it emulsifies.

Drizzle over the slaw and toss well.

Wild Rice Salad

Wild rice is not a rice at all. It's the seed of a wetland grass native to North America. But whatever the name, it adds a nutty flavour and chewy texture to this special salad.

Serves 2.

150 g (1 cup) cooked chickpeas or soybeans

100 g (½ cup) raw wild rice

2 cups (16 fl oz) water

1 medium-sized sweet potato, diced

1 small head broccoli, cut into florets

100 g (3½ oz) snowpeas (mange-tout)

100 g (3½ oz) cherry tomatoes, halved

¼ cup roughly chopped coriander (cilantro) leaves

a handful of beansprouts, to serve

Chilli-Lime Dressing

¼ cup sweet chilli sauce

juice of 1 lime

2 tablespoons vegetable oil

1 tablespoon light soy sauce

1 teaspoon honey, optional

Preheat the oven to 220°C/425°/gas mark 7. Prepare a baking tray by lining with greaseproof paper.

Put the rice and water into a medium-sized saucepan over a medium heat. Bring to the boil then reduce heat to low, cover, and simmer until the grains start to open. This may take anywhere between 25 minutes and 1 hour, depending on how the rice was grown and processed. Add more water during cooking if it becomes too dry, and drain any excess water at the end. Remove from the heat and allow to cool a little.

Meanwhile, peel the sweet potato and cut it into large dice. Put the sweet potato on the baking tray and roast it for 25 minutes, or until the outside is starting to get crunchy and caramelised.

Steam the broccoli and snow peas in a vegetable steamer over rapidly boiling water until tender, about 10 minutes for broccoli and 2 minutes for peas. Rinse with cold water to preserve the colour.

Place the chickpeas, wild rice, pumpkin, broccoli, snow peas, tomatoes and chopped coriander in a large serving bowl and mix well. Drizzle with the dressing and garnish with beansprouts.

To make the Lime-Chilli Dressing, put all the ingredients in a small bowl and whisk to combine.

Tip

Use leftover cooked white or brown rice as a base for a substantial salad. Add peas, corn, red capsicum (bell pepper), parsley, salt and pepper, and lemon juice.

Spinach and Soybean Salad

Of all the beans and legumes, soybeans have the highest protein. They can be cooked ahead for this crunchy salad.

Serves 2 generously.

½ cup cooked soybeans

baby spinach leaves, washed

1 small carrot, grated

1 small red capsicum (bell pepper), sliced lengthwise

1 celery stalk, thinly sliced

a handful of beansprouts

Garlic Dressing

2 tablespoons olive oil

2 tablespoons vinegar

2 garlic cloves, finely chopped

sea salt and cracked black pepper to taste

To make the Garlic Dressing put all the ingredients in a small screw-top jar and shake well so the ingredients and flavours blend.

Toss the soybeans, spinach, carrot, capsicum, celery and sprouts into a bowl, drizzle with dressing and toss well to coat the vegetables. Start crunching.

Spicy Tofu and Rice Salad

Some like it hot. If you're one of them, use more chillies or add sweet chilli sauce at the end.

Serves 2.

10 g (⅓ oz, a large pinch) dried arame

1 tablespoon vegetable oil

1 garlic clove, finely chopped

1 red chilli, seeds removed and finely chopped

2 tablespoons hoisin sauce

400 g (14 oz) firm tofu, cut into bite-sized pieces

1 cup cooked brown rice, kept warm

1 tablespoon chopped cashews (optional)

Put the arame into a small bowl, pour on boiling water and let stand for 10 minutes. Drain and cool.

Warm the wok over a medium heat. Add the oil, garlic, chilli and hoisin sauce and fry gently for a minute, until fragrant. Add the tofu and stir to coat with sauce. Cook until browned on all sides, about 5 minutes.

Combine the warm brown rice, tofu, arame and cashews in a medium-sized bowl. Serve warm.

Japanese Green Tea Noodle Salad

Keep your cool on hot nights by cooking the noodles in the morning.

Serves 2.

100 g (4 oz) Japanese green tea noodles

10 g (⅓ oz, a large pinch) dried arame

½ continental cucumber, very thinly sliced

a handful of beansprouts

1 tablespoon grated fresh ginger

1 tablespoon sesame seeds

Japanese Dressing

3 tablespoons rice vinegar

2 tablespoons tamari

2 tablespoons mirin

1 teaspoon brown sugar

a pinch of salt

Bring a large pot of water to the boil. Add the noodles and stir. Return to the boil, then reduce the heat to medium–high. Cook for 5–8 minutes, or until noodles are tender but firm to the bite. Drain and rinse well in cold water.

Put the arame into a small bowl, add boiling water and stand for 10 minutes. Drain and cool.

To make the Japanese Dressing, combine all ingredients in a small bowl and stir until the sugar and salt have dissolved.

Toss the noodles, arame, cucumber, beansprouts, ginger and sesame seeds into a serving bowl and combine. Pour the dressing over the salad and stir again.

Facing page: Japanese Green Tea Noodle Salad (recipe this page).

Beetroot and Buffalo Salad

Don't freak. I'm talking about the mozzarella made with milk from these beautiful beasts. If you can't find buffalo mozzarella, use bocconcini. Just use red beetroot in place of the golden if you can't find the latter.

Serves 2.

250 g (9 oz) baby red beetroot (beets)

250 g (9 oz) baby golden beetroot (beets)

handful sorrel leaves or any salad leaf of your choice

250 g (9 oz) buffalo mozzarella balls

50 g (¼ cup) roughly chopped walnuts

finely chopped chives

2 tablespoons red wine vinegar

1 tablespoon olive oil

sea salt and cracked black pepper to taste

Scrub the beetroot well, trim the stalk but do not remove. Cover with water in a medium saucepan and bring to the boil, then simmer for 40–45 minutes, or until tender. Remove from the heat, run under cold water and peel off the skin and cut into quarters.

Cut the cheese into quarters, about the same size as the beetroot. Make a bed of sorrel leaves on a serving plate (or 4 individual plates), then toss on beets and cheese. Sprinkle with walnuts and chives. Drizzle with vinegar and oil and season to taste with salt and pepper.

41

Facing page: Beetroot and Buffalo Salad (recipe this page).

Quinoa Salad

A lovely nutty salad with a pink blush from the beetroot. For a change, try it with mint or coriander in place of parsley and finely chopped zucchini and red capsicum instead of the carrot and celery.

Serves 2–4.

1 cup quinoa

2 cups (16 fl oz) boiling water

a pinch of sea salt

1 medium-sized beetroot (beet), grated

1 medium-sized carrot, grated

1 celery stalk, sliced thinly

a handful of chopped parsley

¼ cup almond meal

¼ cup sesame seeds

4 tablespoons lemon juice

2 tablespoons extra-virgin olive oil

sea salt and cracked black pepper to taste

Place the quinoa in a medium-sized heavy-based saucepan and dry-fry on medium–high for a minute or two, until the grains start popping and smell nutty. Stir so the grains toast evenly.

In another saucepan, boil the water with a pinch of sea salt and add the toasted quinoa. Return to the boil. (Don't add the boiling water to the hot saucepan as it will splutter furiously.)

Simmer for 10–12 minutes, stirring often, until the quinoa absorbs all the water. Remove from the heat and allow the quinoa to cool.

In a medium-sized serving bowl, combine the quinoa with the grated vegetables, almond meal, seeds and parsley. Drizzle with lemon juice and oil and toss well to combine. Season to taste with salt and pepper and serve.

Potato Salad

A 'bring a plate' favourite. Choose waxy potato varieties such as kipfler or Tasmanian pink-eye, or use whole chats (small new potatoes).

Serves 4

1 kg (2 lb) waxy potatoes

500 g (1 lb) sugar peas, strings removed

½ cup chopped mint

¼ cup toasted pinenuts

Yoghurt–Mustard Dressing

2 tablespoons lemon juice

2 tablespoons seeded mustard

1 tablespoon yoghurt

1 tablespoon olive oil

1 teaspoon honey

Steam the whole potatoes in a vegetable steamer over rapidly boiling water until tender (15–20 minutes, or until a skewer stuck into the flesh meets little resistance). Allow the potatoes to cool a little, then peel the skin and cut into even chunks.

Blanch the sugar peas by cooking in boiling water for a few minutes. Drain and refresh in cold water.

Toss the potatoes and peas into a large serving bowl.

To make the Yoghurt–Mustard Dressing, mix the lemon juice, seeded mustard, yoghurt, olive oil and honey together in a small bowl until well combined.

Add the dressing to the vegetables and mix until evenly covered. Sprinkle with mint and pinenuts and serve.

Pumpkin and Pecan Salad

The crunch of the pecans goes wonderfully with the sweet tenderness of the pumpkin and couscous.

Serves 2.

500 g (1 lb) pumpkin, peeled and diced

1 cup (8 fl oz) Stock (see page 56)

110 g (½ cup) uncooked couscous

1 small piece ginger, peeled and grated

rocket (arugula) leaves, washed

¼ cup roughly chopped pecan nuts

2 tablespoons balsamic vinegar

1 tablespoon olive oil

sea salt and cracked black pepper to taste

Steam or roast the pumpkin until tender.

Heat the stock until boiling.

Place the couscous and grated ginger into a medium-sized bowl and pour the stock over. Cover and let stand for 5 minutes.

Toss the cooked pumpkin, couscous, rocket and nuts into a large serving bowl and stir to combine. Drizzle with balsamic vinegar and olive oil and season to taste with salt and pepper. Serve warm or cold.

Roast Pumpkin Salad

Brighten the darkest winter days with this warm, colourful salad.

Serves 4.

600 g (20 oz) butternut pumpkin

4 small beetroot (beets)

1 brown onion

2 tablespoons olive oil

2 garlic cloves, finely chopped

sea salt and cracked black pepper to taste

¼ cup pepitas (pumpkin seeds)

baby spinach leaves, well washed

1 tablespoon raspberry vinegar (or red wine vinegar)

Preheat the oven to 200°C/400°F/gas mark 6. Line a large baking tray with greaseproof paper.

Peel the pumpkin, beetroot and onion and cut into wedges.

Mix together the oil, garlic, salt and pepper in a large bowl until well combined. Toss in the pumpkin, beetroot and onion and stir well to coat.

Spread the vegetables on to the baking tray and place in oven for 45–50 minutes, or until the pumpkin starts to brown.

Place the pepitas in a dry frying pan over a medium and fry for a couple of minutes, stirring, until the seeds start to pop and brown.

Combine the roasted vegetables, pepitas and spinach in a large bowl drizzle with raspberry vinegar. Serve warm.

The Earl of Sandwich probably had no idea how he was to revolutionise culinary culture with his idea of slapping two thick slabs of bread with a chunk of meat in-between. I wonder if he'd roll up for one of my creations?

Sandwiches & Roll-Ups

Lettuce Wraps

Sometimes bread can be too heavy, so here's a smart compromise. But don't pack them in a lunchbox: these don't travel well.

Makes 2.

2 whole iceberg lettuce leaves

1 tablespoon tahini, or mayonnaise mixed with Dijon-style mustard

½ avocado, sliced

¼ cucumber, thinly sliced

½ carrot, grated

½ beetroot (beet), grated

a handful of beansprouts

1 teaspoon lemon juice

sea salt and cracked black pepper to taste

Drizzle a little tahini into the centre of each leaf. Fill each leaf with avocado, cucumber, carrot, beetroot, and beansprouts. Drizzle with lemon juice and season to taste with salt and pepper. Roll and eat. Fold in either end then roll up to enclose filling.

Rice-paper Rolls

Once you've mastered the art of rolling these, you could get yourself a job making Cuban cigars!

18 cm (7 in) rice-paper wrappers

any or all of the following, cut into long, thin matchsticks:

cucumber

red capsicum (bell pepper)

firm tofu

carrot

vermicelli, soaked in warm water until pliable

beansprouts

snowpeas (mange-tout)

mint or Vietnamese mint leaves, roughly chopped

coriander (cilantro) leaves, roughly chopped

hoisin or sweet chilli sauce, for dipping

Briefly dip one rice-paper wrapper into warm water until soft and pliant, remove and dry on absorbent paper or a clean tea towel. Alternatively, place a wrapper on a clean, flat surface and brush liberally with warm water. Let it stand for 2 minutes before laying another wrapper on top and repeating process until all the wrappers are soft. Keep a bowl of warm water mixed with lemon juice nearby to dip your fingers so they don't become sticky.

When the wrappers are softened, pile your favourite combination of ingredients down the centre of a wrapper, ensuring that the stack is even and that you have left space on each side. Fold one end of the wrapper over the filling, turn in the sides to hold the vegies in place, then roll up tightly. Don't fold the wrapper over itself too many times as it will become chewy.

Cover the rolls with a slightly damp cloth while making the other rolls. Serve immediately.

49

Toasted Fruit Sandwiches

While Vegemite sandwiches are pretty close to perfect, here are some unusual combos that will get your tastebuds going.

Makes 2 sandwiches.

Banana

1 banana

1 tablespoon sultanas (golden raisins)

$\frac{1}{8}$ teaspoon ground nutmeg

4 slices bread

> Mash the banana in a shallow bowl, add the sultanas and nutmeg and mix well.
>
> Divide mixture between two slices of bread and cover the filling with remaining slices. Lightly press the sandwiches together.
>
> Place in a sandwich-maker, under the grill or in a lightly greased frying pan and toast both sides.

Apple

1 Granny Smith apple

1 tablespoon lemon juice

4 slices bread

1 tablespoon apple butter or jelly

> Peel and grate the apple and combine with the lemon juice. Drain, if too juicy.
>
> Spread half the apple butter over a slice of bread and spoon on the grated apple. Top with another slice of bread. Repeat for the second sandwich. Lightly press the sandwiches together and toast as above.

Cream Cheese and Celery

4 slices bread

1 tablespoon cream cheese

1 celery stalk, very finely sliced

1 tablespoon sultanas (golden raisins)

Spread one slice of bread with half the cream cheese. Place half the celery slices and sultanas on top and cover with another slice of bread. Repeat for second sandwich. Lightly press sandwiches together and toast as above.

Triathlete's Sanga

Sunday is bike ride day for my triathlon squad, and you can be gone for hours. You need food that's easy to carry and can be eaten while riding. This sanga is guaranteed to fuel any flagging body, but you don't have to be a triathlete to enjoy it. At home, add a drizzle of lemon juice and some shredded coconut, and dust with nutmeg and cinnamon.

Makes 2 sandwiches.

2 bananas

4 slices fresh bread, crusts removed

2 tablespoons sultanas (golden raisins)

Peel the bananas and place each on a slice of bread. Sprinkle half the sultanas on each and place a second piece of bread over the filling. Gently compress the sandwich between your hands. Pack into a zip-lock bag (plastic clingwrap is a nightmare to unwrap while cycling).

Eat one-handed while riding along the designated road.

Sushi Rolls

It's fantastic to watch sushi masters at work but it's more fun to have a go yourself. Serves 4.

Sushi Rice

1½ cups sushi rice

2 cups (16 fl oz) water

4 tablespoons rice vinegar

2 tablespoons sugar

2 teaspoons sea salt

Sushi Filling

1 cup (8 fl oz) water

a pinch of sea salt

½ cucumber, cut into batons

½ carrot, cut into batons

8 nori sheets

½ cup sesame seeds

1 avocado, cut into batons

375 g (12½ oz) spiced tofu, cut into batons

50 g (1½ oz) pickled ginger

tamari, for dipping

wasabi to taste

bamboo sushi rolling mat

To prepare the rice, add the rice to 2 cups (16 fl oz) water in a heavy-based saucepan and bring to the boil over a medium heat. Reduce heat to low and simmer, covered, for 20 minutes.

Remove from heat and allow to cool, covered, for 10 minutes. Transfer rice to a large shallow casserole dish and cool to room temperature.

Meanwhile, combine vinegar, sugar and salt in a small bowl and stir until well combined. Pour mixture over cooled rice and stir through with a rice paddle or large wooden spoon.

To make the rolls, mix 1 cup (8 fl oz) water and a pinch of sea salt in a small bowl and stir until salt has dissolved. Place cucumber and carrot in the salted water for a few minutes to soften. Drain.

Toast the nori sheets by waving the shiny side over a high flame for a few minutes until they turn green and become fragrant and crisp.

Toast the sesame seeds in a dry heavy-based saucepan, stirring frequently until golden brown. Set aside.

Put one nori sheet on the bamboo mat. Set up a small bowl of cold water nearby.

Keeping fingers moist, spread rice in a thin layer over nori sheet, extending right to the edges, leaving 5 cm (2 in) of nori uncovered at the far end. Sprinkle rice with toasted sesame seeds. Near the closest edge, stack the avocado, cucumber, carrot, tofu and pickled ginger in a thin horizontal layer. Don't build too high – think long and low.

Holding the ingredients in place with your fingers, begin to roll up the nori sheet, using the bamboo mat to keep everything in place. Gently press the bamboo mat around the nori roll to secure and shape it. Allow the roll to rest for a minute or two before removing mat. Use a wet knife to cut the roll in half.

Repeat using remaining ingredients.

Soups are not only incredibly warming but calming as well because the digestive system isn't required to break down large, complex foodstuffs. Vitamins, minerals and nutrients are absorbed quickly and easily, giving you instant energy.

Soups

Stock

It's so easy to make your own stock – plus it's a great way to use up things like vegetable peel (other than potato), carrot tops and bottoms, onion skins and the skinny inner stalks of celery.

Start by saving well-washed vegetable peel in a plastic bag in the freezer. Keep adding to the bag until you have enough to fill a large pot – ideally a heavy-based 10-litre stockpot.

Add about 2 litres (4 pints) of water to the pot, or enough to cover the vegetables well, plus a bay leaf and some black peppercorns. Simmer, covered, over a low heat for 1–2 hours. Strain and freeze in small portions (about 1 cup/8 fl oz) and you'll be able to rustle up soup in a jiffy.

• If you run out of stock and the soup mood strikes, make do with water, a teaspoonful of soy sauce, miso paste or Vegemite, and a bay leaf.

Facing page: Rice-paper Rolls (recipe page 49).

Kate's Green Soup

Home from the movies one wintry night, my friend Kate peers into the fridge and says, 'What can I eat?' Remembering the peas and zucchini in there, I say, 'Have some tea, and I'll make soup.' She flops on couch, flicking through mags, while I chuck things into a pot. Before long, she has a piping hot bowl of soup in front of her. 'How'd you do that?' she asks. Easily. But I don't tell her that. You can't tell your friends everything, surely.

Serves 2 generously.

200 g (1 cup) green split peas

2 tablespoons olive oil

1–2 garlic cloves, finely chopped

1 green chilli, finely chopped

1 onion, diced

sea salt and cracked black pepper to taste

1 zucchini (courgette), grated, or 1 small head broccoli, chopped

100 g (3½ oz) fresh or frozen green peas

2 cups (16 fl oz) Stock (see page 56)

2 cups (16 fl oz) water

2 tablespoons yoghurt

Rinse the split peas until the water runs clear. Set aside.

Warm the oil in a large heavy-based saucepan over a medium heat. Gently fry the garlic, green chilli and onion until fragrant. Season to taste with sea salt and pepper.

Toss in the zucchini and fresh and dried peas. Stir to coat with oil then add the stock and water and bring to the boil. Reduce the heat and simmer gently, covered, for 25–30 minutes.

Remove from the heat, allow to cool a little, then blend until thick and smooth.

To serve, pour into bowls, and swirl in the yoghurt.

57

Facing page: Reggie's Spinach and Feta Filo Parcels (recipe pages 148–49).

Gazpacho

This will cool your jets in the hotter months. A friend of mine will only eat it with hot pepper sauce and vodka added! To make a super-smooth dinner-party version, roast and skin the red capsicum and peel the tomatoes before blending.

Serves 4.

1 red onion

5 Roma tomatoes

2 medium-sized red capsicum (bell pepper)

1 continental cucumber, peeled

6 basil leaves

1 garlic clove

1 red chilli, seeds removed (optional)

2 tablespoons red wine vinegar

1 tablespoon olive oil

sea salt and cracked black pepper to taste

4 slices sourdough bread to serve

Roughly chop the onion, tomatoes, capsicum, cucumber and basil leaves. Throw them into the bowl of a food processor, along with the garlic and chilli, if using, and blend until coarse. Depending on the size of your food processor, you may need to do this in batches. Pour in the vinegar and oil and blend until well combined. To make a thinner soup, add a cup of water or stock. Season to taste with salt and pepper, then refrigerate for a couple of hours so flavours blend.

To serve, put a slice of sourdough bread in each bowl before pouring in the soup. (That's what's called a sop.)

Carrot and Tangelo Soup

A light and tangy soup. If you don't have tangelos, use oranges instead.

Serves 2.

4 large carrots, peeled and grated

1–2 tablespoons olive oil

⅛ teaspoon ground nutmeg

sea salt and cracked black pepper to taste

1 cup (8 fl oz) water

1 cup (8 fl oz) freshly squeezed tangelo juice (about 2 tangelos)

1 tablespoon chopped mint leaves

Warm a medium-sized heavy-based saucepan over a medium heat, then add olive oil. Gently cook the grated carrots, stirring, until softened. Add the nutmeg and salt and pepper to taste. Add the water and tangelo juice, cover, and simmer on a low heat for about 20 minutes.

Remove from the heat and allow to cool for a few minutes, then blend, process or purée the mixture until smooth-ish.

Return to saucepan and warm through again. Stir in chopped mint and serve.

Apple Soup

Sounds a bit unusual . . . just wait for the taste.

Serves 4.

¼ cup (2 fl oz) good olive oil or 3 tablespoons butter

3 Granny Smith apples, peeled and diced

3 large brown or yellow onions, peeled and diced

1 litre (2 pints) Stock (see page 56)

1 litre (2 pints) non-alcoholic apple cider

sea salt and cracked black pepper to taste

4 tablespoons cream (optional)

Warm a large saucepan over a low heat and add olive oil. Gently cook the apples and onions for about 30 minutes, without browning, stirring often. The longer and slower you cook them, the sweeter the flavour.

Add a little of the stock, then blend the mixture until smooth. Return the mixture to the saucepan and add the remaining stock and cider. Simmer on a low heat for 10 minutes, stirring often. If you are using cream, stir it in and warm through. Season to taste with salt and pepper and serve with crusty white bread.

Fragrant Rice Soup

A simple soup that provides nourishment and peace.

Serves 2.

1 tablespoon olive oil

2 garlic cloves, finely chopped

½ fresh red chilli, finely chopped

1 small piece ginger, peeled and grated

¼ cup raw white rice

1 litre (2 pints) water

1 tablespoon miso paste

sea salt and cracked black pepper to taste

¼ cup chopped fresh parsley

Heat oil in a medium-sized heavy-based saucepan. Gently cook the garlic, chilli and ginger for 1 minute. Add rice and stir to coat the grains in oil, then add water and miso paste. Season to taste with salt and pepper.

Bring to the boil then reduce heat to low and simmer for 30 minutes, stirring occasionally. If you want a thinner consistency, add more water. Before serving, stir in chopped parsley.

Vegetable Miso Soup

My answer to chicken soup: a reviving bowl full of vitamins and minerals.

Serves 2–4.

8 fresh or dried shiitake mushrooms

10 g (⅓ oz, a large pinch) dried arame

50 g (1½ oz) rice vermicelli noodles

50 g (1½ oz) snowpeas (mange-tout)

1 tablespoon sesame oil

1 leek, finely chopped

½ celery stalk, finely chopped

1 carrot, peeled and grated

3–4 tablespoons miso paste

1.25 litres (2½ pints) Stock (see page 56)

1 small piece ginger, peeled and grated

100 g (3½ oz) firm tofu, diced, or fried bean cake or puffs, diced

dried fried shallots to serve

If using dried mushrooms, soak in hot water for 15–20 minutes, then drain and squeeze out water. Remove and discard the stalks and slice the caps finely.

Soak the arame in hot water for 10 minutes. Drain.

Cook the noodles in boiling water for 3 minutes. Drain.

Remove strings from snowpeas and blanch them in boiling water for 1 minute. Refresh in cold water. Drain, and cut into thin diagonal slices.

In a large saucepan, heat the sesame oil over a medium heat and gently fry the leek, celery and carrot. When vegetables start to soften, add the miso paste, stock and ginger and bring to the boil. Reduce heat to low, add the mushrooms, arame, noodles and tofu. Stir to mix and simmer for a minute. Add the snowpeas and allow to warm through. Ladle soup into bowls and sprinkle with dried fried shallots.

Cauliflower and Tofu Soup

Smooth and creamy yet still light and fresh, this doubles as a tonic. If you've been over-indulging, leave out the beans.

Serves 2 generously.

1 medium-sized cauliflower, cut into pieces

150 g (5 oz) silken tofu

500 ml (16 fl oz) Stock (see page 56)

200 g (1 cup) cooked cannellini beans

chopped parsley to taste

sea salt and cracked black pepper to taste

Steam the cauliflower in a vegetable steamer over rapidly boiling water until tender, about 15 minutes.

Blend the cauliflower, tofu and half the stock in a food processor. Add the cannellini beans and the remaining stock and blend until smooth.

Reheat the soup in medium-sized saucepan, adding the parsley and salt and pepper to taste. Serve hot.

Cashew and Celery Soup

I got the inspiration for this calming soup while staying in an ashram in India. If you don't have any celery, use leek.

Serves 2.

2 tablespoons ghee or vegetable oil

100 g (about 1 cup) cashews

4 celery stalks, diced

1 medium-sized potato, diced

1 litre (2 pints) water or Stock (see page 56)

sea salt and cracked black pepper to taste

Heat ghee or oil in a heavy-based saucepan over medium heat and cook the cashews and celery until the cashews start to soften and brown.

Add the potato and water or stock and cook on medium heat for 30 minutes, or until vegetables and nuts are soft. Season to taste with salt and pepper.

Remove from the heat and allow to cool for a few minutes, then blend until smooth. Serve hot.

Pear and Parsnip Soup

Another slightly unusual marriage but you will be rewarded for taking a chance.

Serves 2.

2 tablespoons olive oil or butter

2 pears, peeled and chopped (Packham are good)

2 parsnips, peeled and chopped

1 leek, chopped

1 litre (2 pints) Stock (see page 56)

sea salt and cracked black pepper to taste

50 g (2 oz) crumbled blue cheese, optional

a handful of croutons (optional)

Warm the oil over low heat in heavy-based saucepan. Sweat the pears, parsnip and leek, stirring often, for about 15 minutes, or until they start to soften. To assist this process, wet some greaseproof paper or brown paper and use it to cover the fruit and vegies.

Add the stock (having removed greaseproof paper!) and bring to the boil. Reduce heat and simmer for 15 minutes, or until ingredients are soft.

Remove from the heat and allow the soup to cool before mashing or blending.

Season to taste with salt and pepper and serve hot, perhaps with blue cheese and croutons.

Sweet Potato and Red Lentil Soup

The lovely colour warms you from the outside. If you like a smoother, creamier consistency, add a potato during cooking or stir in silken tofu or yoghurt at the end.

Serves 4.

1 tablespoon olive oil

1 onion, diced

2 garlic cloves, finely chopped

1 bay leaf

2–3 large sweet potato, peeled and diced

1 cup red lentils, washed

1.5 litres (3 pints) Stock (see page 56)

sea salt and cracked black pepper to taste

sprinkling sweet Hungarian paprika (optional)

Warm oil in a large saucepan over a medium heat. Add onion, garlic and bay leaf and fry for a few minutes, until onion softens. Add the sweet potato, lentils and stock and bring to the boil. Simmer, covered, for about 30 minutes, or until soft and cooked. Season to taste with salt and pepper.

Mash or blend to the required consistency and serve hot, sprinkled with paprika.

Beetroot Soup

Beetroot is a great blood cleanser, making this good medicine after a big night. Remember to take off your white T-shirt before you start.

Serves 2.

3 large beetroot (beets), peeled and diced

1 white onion, diced

1 carrot, peeled and diced

1 celery stalk, diced

1 litre (2 pints) Stock (see page 56)

sea salt and cracked black pepper to taste

a small handful of chopped parsley

$\frac{1}{4}$–$\frac{1}{2}$ cup (2–4 fl oz) lemon juice (about 3 lemons)

2 tablespoon light sour cream or yoghurt

Into a large heavy based saucepan, toss the beetroot, onion, carrot and celery and pour in the stock. Bring to the boil, then simmer for 45 minutes, until the vegetables are soft. Season to taste with salt and pepper and towards the end of cooking, stir in the parsley.

Remove from heat and allow to cool a little before processing to desired consistency. (It will not become super-smooth.) Stir in the lemon juice and serve hot or cold with a dollop of sour cream or yoghurt.

Jerusalem Artichoke Soup

Jerusalem artichokes are confusing things: they are neither artichokes nor from Jerusalem. They are, in fact, the roots of a sunflower-like plant. They can cause gas, so avoid eating this the night before an important date, the ballet or a job interview.

Serves 2.

2 tablespoons olive oil

1 leek, chopped

1 garlic clove, finely chopped

500 g (1 lb) Jerusalem artichokes, peeled and diced

1 litre (2 pints) Stock (see page 56)

sea salt and cracked black pepper to taste

a small handful of chopped parsley

Heat oil in a heavy-based saucepan over a medium heat. Gently fry the leek, garlic and artichokes for a few minutes, until the vegetables begin to soften, then add the stock and bring to the boil. Reduce the heat and simmer until the artichokes are tender. Season to taste with salt and pepper.

Remove from the heat and allow to cool a little before blending. Stir in the parsley and serve hot.

Joffa's Pumpkin Soup

When I first met my boyfriend, he had a shed full of pumpkins – all 82 grown that year in his suburban backyard. No wonder his soup is so good.

Serves 4.

1 tablespoon olive oil

1 large carrot, diced

2 medium-sized onions, diced

4 garlic cloves, finely chopped

1 teaspoon curry powder

1 kg (2 lb) pumpkin, diced

2 medium-sized potatoes, diced

2 vegetable stock cubes

2 litres (4 pints) stock

sea salt and cracked black pepper to taste

½ cup (4 fl oz) white rice

4 tablespoons yoghurt (optional)

Heat the oil in a large heavy-based saucepan over medium heat and gently fry the carrot, onion, garlic and curry powder, until the vegies start to soften. Add the cubed pumpkin and potato and fry gently for a minute to coat with oil. Crumble the stock cubes into the stock and bring to the boil.

Reduce the heat to low and simmer for an hour, then add the uncooked rice. Continue simmering for another hour, until the vegies are soft.

Remove from the heat, allow to cool a little, then blend until smooth. Season to taste with salt and pepper.

Pour into bowls and serve hot, perhaps with a dollop of yoghurt.

Laksa

My interpretation of a Malaysian classic. To speed things up, use 2 tablespoons of commercial red curry or laksa paste rather than making your own.

Serves 2.

Laksa Paste

1 red onion

1–2 garlic cloves

1–2 bird's eye chillies, roughly chopped

1 lemongrass stalk, white part only

1 small piece fresh ginger or galangal

small bunch fresh coriander (cilantro), leaves and stalks

1 teaspoon brown sugar

1 teaspoon cumin seeds

2 tablespoons tomato paste

1 tablespoon lime or lemon juice or rice vinegar

1 tablespoon oil

sea salt and cracked black pepper to taste

Soup

1 litre (2 pints) Stock (see page 56)

8 beans, cut in half diagonally

1 medium-sized carrot, peeled and thinly sliced

50 g (1½ oz) dried rice vermicelli noodles

4 tofu puffs

200 g (7 oz) deep-fried tofu, chopped into bite-sized pieces

1 cup (8 fl oz) coconut milk

¼ cucumber, thinly sliced

a handful of beansprouts

a small handful of fresh coriander (cilantro) leaves

4 leaves Vietnamese mint

2 tablespoons dried fried shallots

To make the Laksa Paste, roughly chop the red onion, garlic, chillies and lemongrass stalk. Put them into the bowl of a food processor with remaining ingredients and blend to a paste. This makes enough for two batches of soup. (Refrigerate remaining paste.)

To make the soup, over a low-medium heat warm half the paste in a large heavy-based saucepan. Pour in the stock and bring to the boil.

Add the beans and carrots and cook for 10 minutes, or until tender. In a separate saucepan, cover rice noodles with water and boil for 3 minutes. Drain.

Add the cooked noodles, tofu puffs and deep-fried tofu, and coconut milk to the vegetables. Stir until well combined and warmed through. To serve, top each bowl with cucumber, beansprouts, coriander leaves, two Vietnamese mint leaves and a few deep-fried shallots.

Roasted Tomato and Chickpea Soup

A fabulously filling soup. For a really intense flavour, add another cup of stock and simmer for an extra 30 minutes. A dash of hot pepper sauce never goes astray either.

Serves 2.

5 Roma tomatoes, halved

8 finely chopped basil leaves or 2 teaspoons dried basil

1 onion, cut into 8 wedges

1–2 garlic cloves, skin on

1 tablespoon olive oil

sea salt and cracked black pepper to taste

300 g (10 oz) cooked chickpeas

1 cup (8 fl oz) Stock (see page 56)

50 g (1½ oz) grated parmesan or crumbled feta cheese (optional)

Preheat oven to 180°C/350°F/gas mark 4. Line a baking tray with foil.

Place tomatoes on a baking tray, cut side up, sprinkling each half with basil. Add the onions and whole garlic cloves, spacing the vegetables evenly. Drizzle with olive oil and season with salt and pepper. Cook for about an hour, until vegies are very soft.

Blend the tomatoes, onion and garlic (discard the skins) until smooth.

In a large saucepan, bring stock to the boil and add the chickpeas and roasted tomato mixture.

Cook on medium heat until chickpeas are warmed through. Season with salt and pepper and pour into bowls. Sprinkle with a little parmesan or feta cheese to serve.

Emergency version: Substitute a can of crushed tomatoes and a can of chickpeas for the roasted tomatoes and boiled chickpeas.

Facing page: Roasted Tomato and Chickpea Soup (recipe this page).

Chestnut Soup

The rich reward of chestnuts is worth the hassle of extracting them from their shells.

Serves 2 generously.

500 g (1 lb) chestnuts in shells (yields 250 g/9 ounces)

1 tablespoon olive oil

1 onion, chopped

1 garlic clove, finely chopped

1 celery stalk, diced

1 potato, diced

1 litre (2 pints) Stock (see page 56)

sea salt and pepper to taste

Remove shells from chestnuts by making an incision on the flat side of each nut with a small sharp knife. Put them in a saucepan covered with cold water and bring to the boil. Simmer for 10 minutes, then remove from heat. Take chestnuts from the water two or three at a time and peel off shell and inner skin. Continue until they are all done. OR carefully make a cut in the chestnut shells and put them in the microwave for 5 minutes, a handful at a time, to loosen the shells. Cool slightly, then peel.

Heat oil in a large heavy-based saucepan over medium heat then gently fry onion, garlic, celery and potato until onion becomes soft and transparent. Add peeled chestnuts and stock and bring to the boil. Reduce heat to low and simmer, covered, for 20 minutes. Remove from heat, cool a little, then blend. Season to taste with salt and pepper.

Slurp beside a raging fire.

Facing page: Stuffed Pumpkin (recipe page 145); Stuffed Red Capsicum (recipe page 146); Stuffed Zucchini (recipe page 147).

There is nothing better than a delicious dip to whet the appetite or to stave off hunger pangs before dinner. But do we have a ruling on double-dipping yet?

Take a Dip

Baba Ghanoush

The essential smoky flavour of this Middle Eastern dip evokes camel trains and the hubbub of a crowded market. Choose medium-sized eggplants that are heavy for their size, with shiny, smooth skin.

Makes 1 cup.

1 medium-sized eggplant (aubergine)

2–3 garlic cloves

a small handful of finely chopped coriander (cilantro) leaves

4 tablespoons lemon juice (about 1½ lemons)

1 tablespoon tahini

1 tablespoon olive oil

sea salt and cracked black pepper to taste

Put the extractor fan on.

Place the eggplant directly over an open flame (low-medium heat) on a gas stove, or on to a barbecue, and let the eggplant 'smoke' and blacken before turning it with tongs. Keep turning the eggplant until it has softened and blackened all over, about 10 minutes. The longer you cook it, the smokier the flavour.

Put the eggplant into a plastic bag or lidded container and allow to cool for a few minutes. (This will help the skin come off easily.) Carefully remove and discard the skin, and put the soft flesh into a food processor. Add the garlic, coriander leaves, lemon juice, tahini and olive oil and blend until a smoothish purée. Adjust lemon juice and tahini to taste. Season with salt and pepper. If you like, you could also add a little ground cumin and coriander.

It's also good with baked potatoes or alongside roasted tomatoes and green salad.

Hummus

Don't skimp on the garlic for this fabulously versatile dip, which can also be used to fill baked potatoes and as a sandwich spread (try it with crisp lettuce, red capsicum and cucumber).

Makes 1 cup.

1 cup dried chickpeas (garbanzo beans)

2–4 garlic cloves, finely chopped

½ cup chopped parsley

3 tablespoons tahini

3 tablespoons lemon juice

2 tablespoons extra-virgin olive oil

1 tablespoon sesame seeds

a sprinkling of paprika

sea salt and cracked black pepper to taste

Soak the chickpeas overnight in cold water. Drain and put them into a medium-sized saucepan covered with fresh water. Cook over a low-medium heat until very soft (40–60 minutes). Drain, reserving about a cup of the cooking liquid.

Place all of the ingredients in the bowl of a food processor and blend, adding enough of the cooking liquid to make a smooth dip. Adjust the lemon juice and tahini to taste and season with salt and pepper. Serve sprinkled with paprika.

Hummus will keep for 3–4 days in the fridge.

Tzatziki

Definitely not to be consumed before a first date! I call this Tzatziki-U-Riki because of the after-effects of the garlic.

Makes 2 cups.

500 g (2 cups) thick yoghurt, such as Greek-style or goat's milk

½ continental cucumber, peeled and grated or finely chopped

½ zucchini (courgette), grated

1 teaspoon sea salt

4 garlic cloves, finely chopped

1 tablespoon lemon juice

1 tablespoon finely chopped mint leaves

Suspend the yoghurt in a fine sieve or muslin bag over a large bowl and put it in the fridge for 2 hours to drain off the whey. This results in a thicker dip.

Spread the grated cucumber and zucchini evenly over a large dish and sprinkle with salt. Leave to stand for 15–20 minutes, then drain off any liquid. Squeeze out any excess liquid with paper towel. (You may like to rinse the salt off first.)

Tip the drained yoghurt into a serving bowl and add the remaining ingredients. Stir well. Store in the fridge until ready to use (it keeps for a few days). Serve with bread and sticks of raw carrot, celery, radish and capsicum.

'Ava Dip

Makes 1 cup.

1 large avocado, peeled

¼ cup chopped fresh dill

juice of 1 lemon

1–2 tablespoons olive oil

sea salt and cracked black pepper to taste

Put the avocado flesh into a small processor or blender. Add the remaining ingredients and blend until smooth. Season to taste with salt and pepper and add more lemon juice or olive oil if required. Keeps overnight (drizzle first with lemon juice). Also great on hot toast.

Guacamole

This old favourite is great with nachos (see page 137), on crusty bread or in a mountain bread roll-up with lettuce and chopped tomato.

Makes 1 cup.

1 large avocado, peeled

2 small tomatoes, chopped

1 small red onion, finely chopped

½ teaspoon hot pepper sauce

1 teaspoon lemon juice

small handful chopped coriander (cilantro) leaves (optional)

Put the avocado flesh into a small processor or blender. Add the remaining ingredients (except coriander) and blend for a minute, but don't make it too smooth. If you don't have a blender, mash the avocado, finely chop the other ingredients and stir until well combined. Serve immediately, perhaps garnished with coriander.

18-Carrot Dip

Makes 2 cups.

1 kg (2 lb) carrots, peeled and chopped

2 teaspoons chopped coriander (cilantro) leaves

¼ teaspoon ground coriander

¼ teaspoon ground cumin

sea salt to taste

Steam the carrots in a steamer over rapidly boiling water until soft, about 15 minutes. Combine all the ingredients in a food processor or small blender. Whiz until smooth. If you don't have a blender, mash thoroughly. For a super-smooth finish, add a dollop of yoghurt, ricotta or silken tofu. Keeps for 3 days in the fridge.

Tapenade

A dish of 101 uses.

Makes ¾ cup.

100 g (1 cup) pitted kalamata olives

4 mushrooms, peeled and stalks removed

1 tablespoon capers, rinsed

2 garlic cloves

1 tablespoon olive oil

2 teaspoons roughly chopped fresh parsley or thyme

sea salt and cracked black pepper to taste

Put all the ingredients into a small blender or food processor and blend until fairly smooth. Put into an airtight container and cover with olive oil. Keeps for 3–4 days in the fridge.

Pita Crackers

Great with dips. Ring the changes by topping with grated parmesan and paprika; lemon pepper; mustard and honey; or cumin and sesame seeds.

2 tablespoons olive oil

2 garlic cloves, finely chopped

sea salt and cracked black pepper to taste

4 slices flat bread, such as pita, mountain or sorj

In a small bowl, combine the oil, garlic and salt and pepper. Brush the mixture evenly over the flat bread (if using pita, split into two circles first) and microwave each slice on HIGH for 1 minute, then allow to cool for 30 seconds, until stiff. Break into chunks. If you don't have a microwave, put the bread on to a baking tray and bake for 6 minutes at 160°C/325°F/gas mark 3 until they are crisp and dry. Or grill for a few minutes on HIGH.

We have the Italians to thank for many things, and these top my list. I'd certainly go hungry a few nights of the week without pasta and pizza dishes in my repertoire.

Pasta & Pizza

Napoli Sauce

I'm told this is a traditional Italian Napoli sauce. Well, it's traditional for one family. Use a decent red wine, one you'd be willing to drink.

Serves 4.

1 tablespoon extra-virgin olive oil

sea salt and cracked black pepper to taste

1 whole red onion, peeled, stalk end cut off and root left intact

2 x 400 g (14 oz) cans crushed tomatoes

1 tablespoon tomato paste

1 glass good red wine

1 tablespoon olive oil

1 whole celery stalk

Warm 1 tablespoon oil in a large heavy-based saucepan over a medium heat. Season to taste with salt and pepper. Place the whole onion in the saucepan and add tomatoes, tomato paste, red wine, another splash of olive oil and celery. Reduce the heat and simmer for 20 minutes. Remove onion and celery and serve over gnocchi or spaghetti, with the rest of the red wine.

Working Girl's Sauce

It's late, you've just got home and you're starving. Here's something you can toss together in minutes.

Serves 2.

200 g (7 oz) dried pasta such as penne

1 tablespoon vegetable oil

1 onion, diced

100 g (about ½ cup) kalamata olives, pitted and roughly chopped

1 tablespoon capers, drained and rinsed

1 x 400 g (14 oz) can crushed tomatoes

a small handful of chopped fresh parsley

sea salt and cracked black pepper to taste

Boil plenty of water in a large saucepan and add spaghetti. Cook until al dente, about 8 minutes.

While pasta is cooking, warm oil in a heavy-based saucepan over medium heat. Add onion and fry gently to soften, stirring often. Toss in olives, capers and crushed tomatoes and cook on high for 5–7 minutes, or until sauce is thick. Stir in chopped parsley and season to taste with salt and pepper.

Drain the pasta, put into bowls and spoon on sauce. Devour – using your best table manners!

Garlic and Chilli Spaghetti

Often the simplest things are the best – and that's certainly true here. A dish to whip up when you are short of time and energy.

Serves 2.

200 g (7 oz) dried spaghetti

¼ cup (2 fl oz) olive oil

2 garlic cloves, finely chopped

2 red chillies, finely chopped (seeds removed if you can't stand the heat!)

a handful of finely chopped parsley

sea salt and cracked black pepper to taste

grated parmesan to serve

Boil plenty of water in a large saucepan and add spaghetti. Cook until al dente, about 8 minutes.

Meanwhile, warm olive oil in a medium-sized saucepan over a low heat. Add garlic and chilli and fry gently for a few minutes. Do not let the garlic brown or it will become bitter. Add the parsley and stir through. Season to taste with salt and pepper.

Drain spaghetti, return to saucepan and pour in garlic mixture. Toss and serve, sprinkled with parmesan.

Perfect Pesto

Stir through rice, slather on bread, spoon over boiled potatoes or roasted vegies or, as tradition would have it, as a pasta sauce.

Serves 4.

1 bunch basil leaves, stalks removed

3 garlic cloves, roughly chopped

½ cup (4 fl oz) extra-virgin olive oil

50 g (1½ oz) pinenuts

50 g (1½ oz) grated parmesan

sea salt and cracked black pepper to taste

Place basil, garlic, oil, pinenuts and parmesan in a small blender and whizz until smooth.

To serve with pasta, save a cup of the pasta cooking water before draining, return to the saucepan and stir in the pesto. If the sauce is too thick and hasn't coated the pasta evenly, add a little of the water and stir again.

The paste will keep in the fridge for several days in an airtight container (pour in a little olive oil to cover and prevent it turning black).

Lazy Person's Pesto

Cook pasta (100 g/3½ oz per person is a good guide) in plenty of water. Drain and place in bowls. Drizzle olive oil over the pasta and toss so pasta is evenly coated.

Top with roughly torn basil leaves, pinenuts and shaved parmesan. Season to taste with salt and pepper.

Minty Fettuccine

I go crazy with the mint in this dish because it has such a fresh taste. Plus it helps with the garlic breath afterwards.

Serves 2.

200 g (7 oz) dried fettuccine

1 tablespoon olive oil

2 garlic cloves, finely chopped

1 leek, chopped

200 g (1 cup) fresh or frozen peas, or shelled broad (fava) beans

a handful of mint leaves, roughly chopped

sea salt and cracked black pepper to taste

1–2 tablespoons yoghurt or cream

shaved parmesan, to serve

Boil plenty of water in a large saucepan and add spaghetti. Cook until al dente, about 8 minutes.

While pasta cooks, warm olive oil in a medium-sized heavy-based saucepan. Add garlic and leek and fry gently for a few minutes, without browning. Stir in the peas and continue to cook for about 5 minutes or until the vegetables are tender.

Remove from the heat and stir in yoghurt. Season to taste with salt and pepper.

Drain the pasta and return it to large saucepan. Add sauce and stir in mint leaves. Serve, sprinkled with a little shaved parmesan.

Facing page: Minty Fettuccine (recipe this page).

Walnut Gremolata

Serves 4.

100 g (3½ oz) shelled walnuts

zest and juice of 1 lemon

1 garlic clove, roughly chopped

1 cup roughly chopped parsley

½ cup (4 fl oz) quality olive oil

sea salt and cracked black pepper to taste

Put the walnuts, lemon zest and juice, garlic, parsley and oil into the bowl of a food processor and blend to a paste. Season to taste with salt and pepper. To serve as a pasta sauce, thin with a little of the pasta cooking water.

Olive Walnut Pesto

Serves 4.

200 g (7 oz) green olives, pitted and rinsed

200 g (7 oz) kalamata olives, pitted and rinsed

1 tablespoon capers

100 g (3½ oz) walnuts, shelled and chopped

zest and juice of 1 lemon

1 garlic clove, roughly chopped

¼ cup (2 fl oz) extra-virgin olive oil

cracked black pepper to taste

50 g (1½ oz) crumbled feta or grated parmesan (optional)

Put all the ingredients in the bowl of a food processor and blend to a chunky paste.

Facing page: Rainbow Lasagne (recipe pages 92–3).

89

Rocketing Spaghetti

A dish of stunning textural sensations. A friend of mine uses four times as much gorgonzola, plus a dash of cream!

Serves 2.

200 g (7 oz) spaghetti

200 g (7 oz) rocket (arugula), washed well and roughly chopped

50 g (1½ oz) gorgonzola or another blue cheese, roughly chopped

½ ripe pear or Granny Smith apple, cored and very thinly sliced

50 g (½ cup) shelled walnuts, roughly chopped

1 teaspoon lemon juice

cracked black pepper to taste

Boil plenty of water in a large saucepan and add spaghetti. Cook until al dente, about 8 minutes. Drain the pasta, saving some of the cooking water.

Return the hot pasta to the saucepan and add the rocket and cheese and stir so rocket wilts and cheese starts to melt, over a low heat. Add a little of the reserved pasta water and continue to stir.

Add the pear and walnuts and stir well and allow to warm through. Drizzle with lemon juice, season to taste with pepper and serve hot.

If you prefer a smoother sauce, melt the cheese with some of the pasta water on a very low heat in a separate saucepan and stir in the pear. Add to the spaghetti and rocket and stir to coat.

Lentil Bolognese

This is a versatile sauce. You can spoon it over spaghetti, potatoes or rice, turn it into lasagne or shepherd's pie, serve it with vegies on the side, or pile it on toast for a Sunday night supper. It's even better the day after you've made it.

Serves 4.

1 tablespoon olive oil

1 leek, chopped

1 celery stalk, diced

1 medium-sized red capsicum (bell pepper), diced

1 garlic clove, finely chopped

1 fresh red chilli, finely chopped (seeds removed, if you can't stand the heat!)

1 bay leaf

2½ cups (500 g / 1 lb) cooked whole brown lentils

2 x 400 g (14 oz) cans crushed tomatoes

1 cup (8 fl oz) Stock (see page 56)

a small handful of chopped parsley

a few fresh oregano leaves, chopped

a few basil leaves, chopped

sea salt and cracked black pepper to taste

Warm oil in a large heavy-based saucepan over medium heat. Gently fry the leek, celery, red capsicum, garlic and chilli, stirring, for a few minutes, until the vegetables start to soften. Add bay leaf, lentils, tomatoes and stock.

Bring to the boil, then reduce heat and simmer for 40 minutes, stirring often to prevent it burning. If you want a thinner sauce, reduce the cooking time or add more stock or water.

Stir in the parsley, oregano and basil towards the end of cooking. Season to taste with salt and pepper.

Rainbow Lasagne

A bit time-consuming to make, but the coloured layers look fantastic and the flavour's a knockout.

Serves 4.

Tomato Sauce

1 tablespoon olive oil

2 onions, chopped

2 garlic cloves, finely chopped

1 red chilli, seeds removed and finely chopped

100 g (½ cup) raw red lentils

1 x 400 g (14 oz) can crushed tomatoes

1 cup (8 fl oz) Stock (see page 56)

6 fresh basil leaves, chopped

Filling

200 g (7 oz) pumpkin

1 medium-sized eggplant (aubergine)

2 medium sized zucchini (courgette)

200 g (7 oz) firm tofu, thinly sliced

2–3 lasagne sheets

sea salt and cracked black pepper to taste

Topping

100 g (1⅓ cups) grated parmesan

50 g (¼ cup) sesame seeds

To make the sauce, warm the olive oil in a large heavy-based saucepan over a medium heat. Add onion, garlic and chilli and fry gently, stirring often, for a minute or two, until onion softens. Add lentils, tomatoes and stock, and simmer, uncovered, for 20 minutes. Season to taste with salt and pepper and stir in the chopped basil.

To make the filling, thinly slice the pumpkin, zucchini and eggplant and grill for a few minutes each side under a grill or on a griddle until softened and browned. OR steam and mash the pumpkin, and thinly slice the zucchini and eggplant and use as is.

Preheat the oven to 200°C/400°F/gas mark 6.

To construct the lasagne, lightly oil a large heatproof rectangular dish, and place one lasagne sheet at the bottom. Spoon in a third of the tomato sauce and cover with half the pumpkin, eggplant, zucchini and tofu in separate layers. Season to taste with salt and pepper. Add another sheet of pasta and repeat the process. Finish with the remaining tomato sauce and cover with the grated parmesan and sesame seeds. Season to taste with salt and pepper. (Alternatively, use 100 g/3½ oz silken tofu mixed with the sesame seeds.)

Bake for about 45 minutes, until golden. Cover it with foil towards the end if the topping browns too quickly.

Potato Gnocchi

One of the great comfort foods. Try this with Perfect Pesto (see page 87) or Napoli Sauce (see page 84).

Serves 4.

3 medium-sized boiling potatoes, such as Pontiac, Desiree or Nicola

1 cup self-raising flour

a pinch of sea salt

plain (all-purpose) flour for kneading

¼ cup (2 fl oz) olive oil

sea salt and cracked black pepper to taste

12 roughly torn basil leaves, to serve

grated parmesan to serve

Boil the whole potatoes, skins on, until tender, 15–20 minutes. Drain and allow to cool slightly before peeling. While still warm, mill the potatoes into a large bowl with a potato ricer or food mill, or push through a fine wire sieve with a wooden spoon.

Sift the flour with the salt, and add, a quarter at a time, to the potatoes, mixing well each time, until the mixture is smooth.

Turn mixture out on to a lightly floured board and knead for 1–2 minutes, then divide the dough into 4 portions. Roll each portion into a long sausage shape, about 2.5 cm (1 in) thick. Slice the rolls into 1.5 cm (½ in) pieces.

Meanwhile, bring a large saucepan of salted water to the boil and when the gnocchi are ready, put them into the water, a quarter batch at a time.

The gnocchi will sink to the bottom, then float. Leave them in for 1 minute, then remove with a slotted spoon. Transfer to a serving bowl, or keep warm in a low oven.

Repeat with the remaining gnocchi.

When all the gnocchi are cooked, drizzle with olive oil, toss and season to taste with salt and pepper. Top with basil leaves and parmesan and serve immediately.

Crunchy Pita Pizza

A substantial snack for those times when you need food in a hurry. They're also great with Tapenade (see page 80) brushed on to the base.

Serves 2.

2–3 tablespoons tomato paste or seeded mustard

1 medium-sized potato

100 g (3½ oz) pumpkin

1 large or 2 mini pita bread

5 garlic cloves, peeled but left whole

50 g (1½ oz) feta, cubed or crumbled

a few sprigs of fresh rosemary

a drizzle of olive oil

sea salt and cracked black pepper to taste

Preheat the oven to 200°C/400°F/ gas mark 6.

Brush the tomato paste on to the pita bread.

Peel the potato and pumpkin and cut them into paper-thin slices. Arrange on the bread in a single layer, with minimal overlapping. Top with garlic cloves, feta and rosemary. Drizzle with olive oil and season to taste with salt and pepper.

Bake for 20 minutes, until the feta is golden-brown and the vegetables have softened.

Mushroom Mini Pizzas

Here's a pizza with a twist: built on a mushroom base.

Serves 2.

4 large field mushrooms

4 thin lengthwise slices zucchini (courgette)

2 Roma tomatoes, sliced

1 tablespoon olive oil

2 tablespoons tomato paste

a few fresh thyme leaves

4 baby spinach leaves, washed and dried

4 slices Gruyère cheese

sea salt and cracked black pepper to taste

Preheat oven to 220°C/425°F/gas mark 7.

Peel the mushrooms and remove the stalks. Brush the mushrooms, zucchini slices and tomatoes with olive oil and bake for 15 minutes, or until they soften and start to brown. Alternatively, brown the mushrooms on a griddle.

Spread the mushroom gills with tomato paste. Sprinkle with thyme and cover each mushroom with a spinach leaf, followed by slices of zucchini, tomato and cheese. Season to taste with salt and pepper and grill for a few minutes, until the cheese starts to melt.

Wholemeal Pizza Base

Use this as the starting point for a million different meals, such as with leftover roasted vegies and chopped garlic.

Makes 1 small thick crust or 1 large thin crust.

7 g (¼ oz/1 sachet) active dry yeast

½ cup (4 fl oz) warm water

2 cups wholemeal flour

a pinch of salt

1 teaspoon brown sugar

½ cup (4 fl oz) warm water

plain (all-purpose) flour for rolling

olive oil for cooking

Dissolve the yeast in the first measure of warm water and set aside.

In a large bowl, sift the flour and add salt and sugar. Pour the yeast mixture and the additional water into the flour and stir until well combined. Turn out on to a lightly floured board and knead for a few minutes, until the dough is smooth and elastic.

Return the dough to the bowl and put in a warm spot for 30 minutes, or until the dough doubles in size. (The yeast grows more quickly in a warm, but not hot, environment.)

Meanwhile, preheat the oven to 215°C/425°F/gas mark 7.

When the dough has risen, roll it out on a lightly floured surface to fit the pizza tray. Brush with a little olive oil and bake for 20 minutes, until golden brown and the bottom sounds hard and hollow when tapped.

Tomato and Garlic Pizza Bread

A substantial pre-dinner nibble or something for the table.

Makes 1.

½ cup (4 fl oz) warm water

7 g (¼ oz/1 sachet) active dry yeast

2 cups self-raising flour

a pinch of salt

1 teaspoon sugar

½ cup (4 fl oz) warm water

plain (all-purpose) flour for rolling

2 tablespoons olive oil

3 cloves garlic, finely chopped

sea salt and cracked black pepper to taste

10 basil leaves

2 ripe tomatoes, cut into 1 cm (⅓ in) slices

Dissolve the yeast in the first measure of warm water and set aside.

In a large bowl, sift the flour and add the salt and sugar. Pour the yeast mixture into the flour and stir until well combined. Turn out on to a lightly floured board and knead for a few minutes, until the dough is smooth and elastic. Return the dough to the bowl and put it in a warm spot for 30 minutes, or until the dough doubles in size.

Meanwhile, preheat the oven to 220ºC/425ºF/gas mark 7.

When the dough has risen, roll it out on a lightly floured board to fit a standard-sized baking tray.

In a small bowl, mix the olive oil, garlic, salt and pepper and brush on the pizza base. Scatter the basil leaves evenly over the base and top with tomato pieces. Bake for 20 minutes, until the base is golden brown and the bottom sounds hard and hollow when tapped. Cut into squares and serve.

Banana and Beans Pizza

It may sound like a wacky combo, but trust me, it works. Mango chutney is a great accompaniment.

Makes 1.

½ cup (4 fl oz) warm water

7 g (¼ oz/1 sachet) active dry yeast

2 cups plain (all-purpose) flour

a pinch of salt

1 teaspoon brown sugar

½ cup (4 fl oz) warm water

plain (all-purpose) flour for rolling

1 banana, sliced

juice of 1 lime

⅓ cup cooked red kidney beans

⅓ cup sultanas (golden raisins)

2 tablespoons vindaloo curry paste

4 tablespoons yoghurt

Dissolve the yeast in the first measure of warm water and set aside.

In a large bowl, sift the flour and add the salt and sugar. Pour the yeast mixture into the flour and stir until well combined. Turn out on to a floured board and knead for a few minutes, or until the dough is smooth and elastic. Return the dough to the bowl and put in a warm spot for 30 minutes, or until the dough doubles in size.

Meanwhile, preheat the oven to 220°C/425°F/gas mark 7.

Roll out the dough thinly on a lightly floured board to fit the pizza tray.

Combine the banana, lime juice, beans and sultanas. Brush the pizza base with vindaloo paste and top with the banana and bean mix. Bake for 20 minutes, until the base is golden brown and the bottom sounds hard and hollow when tapped. Allow to cool slightly before dolloping on yoghurt.

99

Once the domain of happy, hippy people, the wonderful world of rice and grains has been embraced by most people – except my dad, who's a dyed-in-the-wool meat-and-three-veg bloke. Despite my best efforts, I can't convert him!

Rice & Grains

Master Risotto

The more you stir, the more the grains rub against each other, the more the starch is released, and the creamier the risotto. Master the basic recipe, then go wild with your own improvisations.

Serves 2.

1.5 litres (3 pints) Stock (see page 56)

2 tablespoons olive oil

1 onion, diced

2 garlic cloves, finely chopped

1½ cups arborio rice

½ cup (4 fl oz) white wine (optional)

1 bay leaf, folded along its spine

sea salt and cracked black pepper to taste

freshly grated parmesan cheese, to serve

Warm the stock in a medium-sized saucepan over a low heat. It doesn't need to be simmering.

In a large heavy-based saucepan, warm the olive oil over a medium heat and add the onion and garlic. Gently fry for a few minutes until the onion starts to soften but not brown.

Add the rice and stir for a couple of minutes or until each grain is coated in oil and looks shiny. If you are using wine, add it now, stirring until the wine has been absorbed.

Add a ladleful of hot stock to the rice and stir constantly until the stock has been absorbed. Repeat, stirring, until all the stock has been used and the rice is al dente (tender but still slightly firm), 20–30 minutes.

Remove the bay leaf, season to taste with salt and pepper, and serve, sprinkled with parmesan.

Variations

Asparagus: Steam asparagus and top cooked risotto with spears. Drizzle with a little lemon juice and olive oil and season with salt and pepper.

Lemon and Thyme: stir in 1 tablespoon fresh thyme when you add the rice. Stir in the zest of a lemon at the end.

Mushroom: finely slice (or chop) mushrooms and add them to the rice halfway through the cooking process. Stir in 1 tablespoon chopped parsley and toasted pinenuts at the end.

Peas and Sage: replace the onion with chopped leek. Stir 1 cup cooked peas and a few fresh sage leaves (not too many as they are very pungent) into the rice halfway through the cooking process.

Roasted vegetables: chop any combination of your favourite vegetables (including, perhaps, red onion, pumpkin, parsnip, carrot, beetroot or sweet potato) into large cubes. Put them in a roasting dish with 1 tablespoon of olive oil and roast in a moderate oven (180°C/350°F/gas mark 4) for 30–40 minutes, or until tender. Stir them into the rice halfway through the cooking process or pile on to the risotto at the end.

Saffron: place several strands of (real) saffron (not saffron powder) in a tablespoon hot water until the colour is released. Stir it into the rice halfway through the cooking process.

Ginger and Lemongrass Risotto

My friend Rodd created this masterpiece, a fusion of East and West. It's an absolute ripper.

Serves 2–3.

1 litre (2 pints) stock

1 tablespoons vegetable oil

1 onion, chopped

1 lemongrass stalk (soft inner part only), finely chopped

1–2 garlic cloves, finely chopped

1 cup arborio rice

½ cup (4 fl oz) shao hsing (Chinese rice wine)

⅓ cup (2½ fl oz) white wine

⅓ cup chopped Chinese pickled ginger

6 water chestnuts, sliced

3–4 kaffir lime leaves, finely chopped

cracked black pepper to taste

⅓ cup (2½ fl oz) coconut cream

chilli jam or sweet chilli sauce, to serve

14 Thai basil leaves, roughly chopped,
      or ½ cup roughly chopped coriander (cilantro) leaves

Warm the stock in a medium-sized saucepan over a low heat. It doesn't need to be boiling, just kept warm.

Heat the oil in a large heavy-based saucepan over a medium heat and gently fry the onion and lemongrass for 3–4 minutes, until the onion softens. Add the garlic and cook for 2 more minutes, without browning. Add the rice and stir to coat with oil for 1 minute. Pour in the rice wine and white wine and stir until absorbed. Add a ladleful of hot stock and continue stirring until absorbed. Repeat, stirring constantly, until all the stock has been used. (If you run out of stock before the rice is cooked, use hot water.)

Halfway through the cooking process (after about 15 minutes) throw in the ginger, water chestnuts, and lime leaves and a little cracked pepper. When the rice is nearly cooked, stir in the Thai basil, reserving some to use as a garnish. When cooked (about 30 minutes), the rice should be tender but still slightly firm.

Remove from the heat and pour the coconut cream over the rice. Cover with foil or a lid. After 2–3 minutes take off the lid, stir in the coconut cream and ladle into bowls. Add a dollop of chilli jam to each bowl and garnish with the Thai basil.

Roasted Pumpkin Orzotto

Orzotto is risotto made from what the Italians call orzo, or pearl barley. It has a nuttier taste and a firmer texture than arborio rice. Here, all the liquid goes in at once, as for a pilaf, but you'll need to visit the kitchen every now and then to rattle the pots.

Serves 2.

1 tablespoon olive oil

500 g (1 lb) pumpkin

2 tablespoons olive oil

1 onion, diced

1 garlic clove, finely chopped

sea salt and cracked black pepper to taste

1 cup pearl barley, rinsed

2 cups (16 fl oz) Stock (see page 56)

½ cup (4 fl oz) water

100 g (4 oz) feta, crumbled

2 generous handfuls roughly chopped rocket (arugula) leaves

Preheat the oven to 180°C/350°F/gas mark 4.

Peel and dice the pumpkin and put it in a large mixing bowl. Pour in the olive oil and stir to coat. Using a slotted spoon, lift the pumpkin out of the bowl and on to a baking tray, draining off the excess oil. Season to taste with salt and pepper. Put the tray in the oven and cook for 40 minutes, until the pumpkin is tender. Towards the end of cooking, put the feta on the tray and allow it to soften and warm through.

Meanwhile, warm the oil in a large heavy-based saucepan over a medium heat. Add the onion, garlic, and salt and pepper to taste, and cook until onion has softened but not browned. Stir in the pearl barley until the grains are evenly coated with oil.

Pour the stock and water into the saucepan and bring to the boil, then reduce heat to low, cover, and simmer. Set the timer for 45 minutes but stir occasionally to prevent the grains from sticking and to check the pumpkin.

When pumpkin is tender, put three-quarters of it into a bowl and mash. Stir it, with the rocket, into the pearl barley until well combined.

Serve immediately, topped with the remaining pumpkin pieces and feta.

Quick idea

Slow-cooked Red Cabbage and Apples

Heat some olive oil over medium heat and add some peppercorns, bay leaves, cloves and salt. Stir until fragrant, then add sliced cabbage leaves and some finely diced Granny Smith apple. Add some water and a splash of apple cider vinegar and a little brown sugar and reduce the heat. Put the lid on and cook until the cabbage is tender. This may take up to an hour.

Moroccan-style Pilaf

While not traditional, this uses all the lovely warm spices of the souk (market).

Serves 2.

2 tablespoons vegetable oil

1 onion, diced

2 medium-sized carrots, diced

2 garlic cloves, finely chopped

½ teaspoon chilli flakes

2 teaspoons ground ginger

2 teaspoons ground cumin

1 teaspoon ground coriander

1 cup basmati rice

¼–½ preserved lemon, finely chopped, or zest of 1 lemon

100 g (4 oz) okra or beans, washed and stalk trimmed, but not chopped

150 g (½ cup) cooked chickpeas

2 cups (16 fl oz) Stock (see page 56)

½ cup chopped coriander (cilantro) leaves

75 g (½ cup) roughly chopped cashews or pistachios

Preheat oven to 180°C/350°F/gas mark 4.

Warm oil in large heavy-based saucepan over a medium heat and add onion, carrot, garlic, chilli flakes, ground ginger, cumin and coriander. Stir until the vegetables start to soften and the spices are fragrant. Add the rice and preserved lemon and cook for a few minutes, stirring, until the rice is coated with spices. Add the okra, chickpeas and stock and bring to the boil.

Pour the mixture into a large ovenproof baking dish and cover with foil or a lid. Bake for 45–50 minutes, or until the liquid is mostly absorbed. Serve sprinkled with coriander leaves and cashews.

Three-pepper Paella

The traffic-light colours make this dish look festive, but you can use any vegetables you have handy. And if you don't have a paella pan, use a large heavy-based saucepan.

Serves 2.

2 tablespoons vegetable oil

1 red onion, diced

2 garlic cloves, finely chopped

1 red chilli, seeds removed and chopped finely

1 cup medium-grain rice

1 red capsicum (bell pepper), diced

1 yellow capsicum (bell pepper), diced

1 green capsicum (bell pepper), diced

2 ripe tomatoes, diced

1 teaspoon paprika

100 g (about ½ cup) kalamata olives, pitted and halved

2 cups (16 fl oz) Stock (see page 56)

Warm the oil in the pan over a medium heat and gently fry the onion, garlic and chilli for a few minutes, until the onion softens. Pour in the rice and stir for a few minutes to ensure the grains are coated with oil. Add the capsicum, tomatoes, paprika, olives and stock and bring to the boil. Reduce the heat to low, cover and simmer for 15 minutes, or until the rice is al dente.

Nutty Couscous

On a bed of steamed bok choy, this makes a lovely and light meal.

Serves 2.

220 g (1 cup) dried couscous

50 g (¼ cup) roughly chopped pistachio nuts

50 g (¼ cup) chopped pecans

50 g (¼ cup) slivered almonds

50 g (¼ cup) sesame seeds

2 cups (16 fl oz) Stock (see page 56)

a small handful of parsley, finely chopped

a small handful of coriander (cilantro) leaves, finely chopped

1 tablespoon olive oil

1 tablespoon white wine vinegar

a squeeze of lemon juice

sea salt and cracked black pepper to taste

Combine the couscous, nuts and sesame seeds in a large heatproof bowl. Mix.

Bring the stock to the boil and pour it over couscous mixture. Cover, and let stand for 5 minutes.

Stir in the parsley and coriander, olive oil, vinegar, and lemon juice. Season to taste with salt and pepper and serve immediately.

Fried Rice

Here's a great way to use up leftover rice that has been in the fridge for a couple of days and anything else that needs to be used – celery, carrot, mushrooms – or just a whole lot of fresh herbs.

Serves 2.

2 tablespoons peanut oil

1 garlic clove, finely chopped

1 small piece ginger, grated

2 cups cooked rice

1 red capsicum (bell pepper), diced

1 cup small pineapple pieces

2 spring onions (scallions), green and white parts, sliced

¼ cup pecan halves

sweet chilli sauce to serve

Warm the oil in a wok over a medium heat and gently fry the garlic and ginger for 1 minute, without browning. Add the rice and capsicum and stir-fry for a few minutes, until capsicum starts to soften. Add the pineapple, spring onions and pecans and warm through. Serve with a drizzle of sweet chilli sauce.

I only have two words for you: comfort food.

Curries & Casseroles

Banana Curry

People may think you've gone troppo when you serve this up, but trust me when I say you'll go ape over the flavour. It looks impressive served on a banana leaf, if you have one.

Serves 2.

1–2 tablespoons oil

1–2 tablespoons red curry paste

1 onion, diced

2 firm bananas, cut into large chunks

200 g (7 oz) firm tofu, diced

100 g (1 cup) peas or chopped beans

¼ cup (2 fl oz) Stock (see page 56)

sea salt and cracked black pepper to taste

¼ cup (2 fl oz) lime juice (about 2)

½ cup (4 fl oz) yoghurt

6 basil leaves, chopped

Warm the oil in a large heavy-based saucepan over a medium heat and gently fry the curry paste and onions for a few minutes, until the onions soften.

Add the bananas, tofu and peas and stir to coat with paste. Pour in the stock and continue to cook until the bananas and peas are tender, about 10 minutes.

Remove from the heat and stir in the lime juice, then the yoghurt. Season to taste with salt and pepper. Garnish with chopped basil and serve, perhaps with basmati rice.

Vegetable Rogan Josh

While this takes some time to cook, it requires very little effort. Make plenty and freeze the rest for later.

Serves 4.

1–2 tablespoons oil

1 onion, diced

2 medium-sized carrots, cut into 1 cm (⅓ in) rounds

2 tablespoons rogan josh paste

2 teaspoons curry powder

2 garlic cloves, finely chopped

3 medium-sized potatoes, cut into large chunks

300 g (10 oz) Brussels sprouts, trimmed and large ones cut in half

1 Granny Smith apple, cubed

¼ cup sultanas (golden raisins)

1 x 400 g (14 oz) can crushed tomatoes

1½ cups (12 fl oz) water

sea salt and cracked black pepper to taste

Warm the oil in a large heavy-based saucepan over a medium heat and gently fry the onion and carrot for about 2 minutes, or until starting to soften.

Add the rogan josh paste, curry powder and garlic and fry gently for 2 more minutes, or until aromatic. Add the remaining ingredients, reduce the heat to low and simmer, covered, for about 30 minutes.

Remove the lid and cook for another 30 minutes, stirring often, until the mixture thickens. Season to taste with salt and pepper and serve on its own or with rice.

Ratatouille

Fantastic on its own, ratatouille also makes a lovely filling for a baked spud, a pasta sauce or a chunky dip with doorstops of fresh bread.

Serves 2.

2 tablespoons olive oil

1 onion, thinly sliced

1 garlic clove, finely chopped

1 medium-sized eggplant (aubergine), cut into large dice

2 medium-sized zucchini (courgette), cut into large dice

1 medium-sized red capsicum (bell pepper), cut into large dice

8 medium-sized mushrooms, cut into quarters

1 x 400 g (14 oz) can crushed tomatoes

1 cup (8 fl oz) Stock (see page 56)

1 bay leaf, folded along the spine

2 teaspoons chopped fresh oregano or 1 teaspoon dried oregano

sea salt and cracked black pepper to taste

Warm the oil in a large heavy-based saucepan over a medium heat and gently fry the onion and garlic for a few minutes, until soft.

Toss in the eggplant and stir to coat with oil. Cook for a few minutes, then add all remaining ingredients. Reduce heat to low and simmer, stirring frequently, for 20–30 minutes, or until vegetables are tender. Remove the bay leaf before serving.

Mushroom Magic

A full-on fungus fest guaranteed to add a little magic to your life! If you can't find all of these, use button mushrooms.

Serves 2.

1 tablespoon peanut oil

1 garlic clove, finely chopped

1 small piece ginger, peeled and finely grated

100 g (3½ oz) oyster mushrooms

100 g (3½ oz) hon shimeji (beech mushrooms)

100 g (3½ oz) fresh shiitake, stalks discarded and caps sliced

100 g (3½ oz) enoki mushrooms

2 tablespoons hoisin sauce

1 tablespoon shao-hsing (Chinese rice wine)

1 tablespoon shoyu

1 teaspoon sesame oil

Heat the oil in a wok over a medium heat. Toss in the garlic and ginger and fry for a minute, without browning. Throw in all the mushrooms and stir-fry for a minute. Combine the hoisin, rice wine, shoyu and sesame oil in a small bowl and stir into the mushrooms. Cover and simmer for 2 minutes, until mushrooms are tender. Serve with brown rice and steamed bok choy.

Vegetable Ragout

A warming dish to ward off winter. The hardest part is chopping the vegies into similar sized bits so they cook evenly.

2 generous serves plus a little more, or 4 serves with rice.

1–2 tablespoons olive oil

1 leek, white part only, diced

1 medium-sized carrot, cut into 1 cm (⅓ in) rounds

1 celery stalk, diced

1–2 garlic cloves, finely chopped

1 red chilli, seeds removed and finely chopped

1 medium-sized potato, diced

1 medium-sized parsnip, diced

1 small sweet potato, diced

1 x 400 g (14 oz) can crushed tomatoes

1 tablespoons tomato paste

2 bay leaves, folded along spine

1 teaspoon dried oregano leaves

1 teaspoon dried basil

hot pepper sauce to taste

sea salt and cracked black pepper to taste

200 g (7 oz) broccoli, roughly chopped

200 g (7 oz) cauliflower, roughly chopped

100 g (3 oz) whole button mushrooms

1 cup (8 fl oz) Stock (see page 56) or water, if necessary

Warm the oil in a large heavy-based saucepan over a medium heat. Gently fry the leek, carrot, celery, garlic and chilli, for about 2 minutes, until vegetables start to soften.

Add the potatoes, parsnip and sweet potato and stir quickly before adding the tomatoes and paste, herbs and a dash of hot pepper sauce. Bring to the boil then reduce heat to low and simmer, covered, for 20 minutes.

Add the broccoli, cauliflower and mushrooms, cover, and simmer for another 20 minutes. Remove the lid and cook, stirring often, until the mixture thickens. If it becomes too thick before the vegies are cooked, add a little stock or water. Serve on its own or with rice or pasta.

Quick idea

Celeriac and Potato Mash

Peel potatoes and celeriac, and cut into large cubes. Place in a large saucepan with water or stock, and bring to the boil. Reduce the heat and simmer for about 20 minutes, or until soft. Drain, save a cup of the cooking water, and mash the vegetables, moistening as necessary. For a creamier consistency, add olive oil or soy drink. Stir in the sesame seeds and parsley. Season to taste with salt and pepper.

Tempeh–Kombu Combo

A delicious rib-sticking stew full of essential vitamins and minerals as well as protein, carbs and good fats. Carrot, swede, turnip, squash, cabbage and potato make equally hearty additions.

Serves 4.

3 kombu strips

200 g (7 oz) butternut pumpkin

200 g (7 oz) cauliflower florets

200 g (7 oz) broccoli florets

1 onion, diced

2 cups (16 fl oz) Stock (see page 56)

1 small piece ginger, peeled and grated

1 tablespoon arrowroot or cornflour (cornstarch)

¼ cup (2 fl oz) cold water

200 g (7 oz) tempeh, cut into strips

olive oil

tamari to taste

Cover the kombu with boiling water and stand for 10 minutes, or until soft. Drain.

Put the chopped pumpkin, cauliflower, broccoli and onion into a large saucepan with the softened kombu, stock and ginger. Bring to the boil over a medium heat, then reduce heat to low and simmer for about 15 minutes, or until vegetables are becoming soft. (To save time, microwave each vegetable separately on HIGH for 1–2 minutes before adding to the saucepan.)

In a small bowl, mix the arrowroot and cold water until smooth, then stir into vegetables until the mixture thickens. Continue cooking until the vegetables are tender, about 10 minutes.

Meanwhile, brush the tempeh with a little olive oil and cook in a wok or frying pan over a medium heat until golden brown.

Spoon the kombu stew into bowls and top with tempeh. Serve immediately, seasoned to taste with tamari. Great with brown rice.

Quick idea

Stir-fried Greens

Use any greens you like – bok choy, broccoli, cabbage, snowpeas (mange-tout). Heat some oil in a wok, add some garlic and chilli, and stir-fry without browning. Add the greens, then some rice wine, cover and cook. Finish with some tamari and sesame seeds.

Tofu Masala

Don't be daunted by the long list of ingredients. It doesn't take long to throw together this dish – and it's worth every second!

Serves 4.

1 red bird's eye chilli, roughly chopped (seeds removed for less fire)

2–4 garlic cloves, roughly chopped

1 small piece ginger, roughly chopped

2 tablespoons roughly chopped coriander (cilantro) leaves

1 tablespoon whole coriander seeds

1 teaspoon whole black peppercorns

1 teaspoon black mustard seeds

1 teaspoon fenugreek

1 teaspoon ground turmeric

1 teaspoon brown sugar

a pinch of sea salt

juice of 1 lemon

1 tablespoon vegetable oil

2 onions, roughly chopped

400 g (14 oz) firm tofu

200 g (7 oz) green beans, cut into 2.5 cm (1 in) lengths

100 g (4 oz) button mushrooms, cut into quarters

4 ripe tomatoes, roughly chopped

Put the chilli, garlic, ginger, coriander leaves, spices, sugar, salt and lemon juice in a food processor or small blender and blend to a paste.

Heat the oil in a large heavy-based saucepan over a medium heat and add the onions. Fry gently for 2 minutes, or until soft. Add the chilli paste and stir until the onion is well coated. Add the tofu and gently stir again. Toss in the beans, mushrooms and tomatoes, reduce the heat to medium and cook for 10 minutes. Reduce the heat to low and continue cooking for another 5 minutes, until the vegetables are tender. Serve with jasmine rice and mango chutney.

To intensify the flavour, combine all the spices from chilli to the fenugreek and dry-fry in a heavy-based saucepan for a minute, or until aromatic. Add sugar, salt and lemon juice and blend to a paste.

Bugs' Delight

Peel and thinly slice some carrots. Heat some olive oil in a pan, add some chopped garlic and ginger, and cumin, paprika and chilli powder to taste. Add the carrots and cook until tender. Add a squeeze of lemon juice. Mix together some yoghurt and coriander leaves and stir through the carrots.

Hearty, rib-sticking food to fill you up and warm you through the wintery months. My motto: use chilli in the chilly months – it's like your own personal central heating.

Bakes & Beans

Spicy Baked Beans

If you've only ever eaten baked beans from the can, you've 'bean' seriously missing out. Try these at brekkie, in a baked potato, or in a toasted sandwich.

Serves 2.

175 g (1 cup) dried beans, such as borlotti, cannellini or haricot

1 tablespoon olive oil

1 onion, diced

1–2 garlic cloves, finely chopped

2 small red chillies, seeds removed and finely chopped

1 celery stalk, finely chopped

1 small red capsicum (bell pepper), finely chopped

1 x 400 g (14 oz) can crushed tomatoes

4 finely chopped semi-dried tomatoes or 1 tablespoon tomato paste

1 cup (8 fl oz) red wine or Stock (see page 56)

1–2 bay leaves

sea salt and cracked black pepper to taste

a small handful of chopped parsley

shaved parmesan to serve

Soak the beans in cold water overnight. The next day, drain the beans and put them in a medium-sized pan, covered with fresh water. Bring to the boil then reduce the heat to low and simmer for 45 minutes, or until tender. Drain.

Heat the olive oil in a large heavy-based saucepan over a medium heat and gently fry the onion, garlic, chilli and celery for a few minutes until the vegetables begin to soften. Add the capsicum, tomatoes, red wine, bay leaves and beans and bring to the boil. Season to taste with salt and pepper. Reduce the heat and simmer on low for an hour, covered, stirring occasionally. If too dry, add a little more red wine or stock.

Towards the end of cooking, stir in the parsley. Sprinkle with shavings of parmesan to serve.

Freekah and Cottage Cheese Pie

Freekah, a green durum wheat grain, has an intriguing nuttiness. But if you can't find it, use rice or barley to make this delish dish, which is fabulous hot or cold, served with salad or steamed vegetables.

Serves 2.

1 cup cooked freekah

1 tablespoon olive oil

1 onion, chopped

1 garlic clove, finely chopped

1 bunch silverbeet (Swiss chard) or spinach, washed, stems removed and leaves finely chopped

250 g (9 oz) cottage cheese or ricotta

2 tomatoes, seeds removed and diced, or 2 semi-dried tomatoes

6 fresh basil leaves

50 g (1½ oz) cheese (feta, Gruyère, mozzarella or parmesan), grated or chopped

sea salt and cracked black pepper to taste

Cook freekah as for steamed rice, using 3 parts water to 1 part freekah.

Preheat the oven to 200°C/400°F/gas mark 6 and lightly grease a shallow pie dish.

In a medium heavy-based saucepan warm the olive oil over a medium heat and gently fry the onion and garlic for a few minutes, until the onion is soft. Add the silverbeet and cook until it has wilted.

Meanwhile, combine the cottage cheese, tomato, basil and cheese in a large mixing bowl. Season to taste with salt and pepper. Stir in the freekah and the silverbeet to combine. Pile the freekah mixture into the pie dish and cook for 45 minutes, or until firm and golden.

Potato and Spinach Pie

A rustic pie perfect for wintery nights.

Serves 4.

Filling

6 medium-sized boiling potatoes, such as Pontiac, Desiree or Nicola

2 tablespoons olive oil

1 bunch spinach, well washed, drained and finely chopped

50 g (¼ cup) pinenuts

1 tablespoon kelp granules

a pinch of sea salt

Rustic Pastry

2 cups wholemeal plain flour

½ cup wheatgerm

2 tablespoons sesame seeds

a pinch of sea salt

½ cup (4 fl oz) olive or rapeseed (canola) oil

½ cup (4 fl oz) chilled water

To make the Filling, steam or boil the whole potatoes (skins on) until tender, 15–20 minutes. Drain and allow to cool slightly before removing skins. Add the olive oil, mash lightly, then stir in the chopped spinach, pinenuts, kelp and salt. Mix well and set aside.

Preheat the oven to 230°C/450°C/gas mark 8.

To make Rustic Pastry, sift the flour into a large mixing bowl and tip in the husks left in the sieve. Stir in the wheatgerm, sesame seeds and salt to mix well. Add the oil and stir until mixture resembles breadcrumbs. Add the water a little at a time and mix to form a firm dough.

Turn the dough out on to a lightly floured board and knead gently. It will be more crumbly than the traditional white flour and butter pastry so you will be pressing it together rather than kneading. The advantage is that you can be quite rough with it and patch it together if necessary.

Divide the pastry into 2 unequal pieces (one third and two thirds). Roll out the larger piece to cover the base of a round 27 cm (10½ in) pie dish. Spoon the filling into the pie case and pack it in well, making a small mound in the centre. Roll out the remaining pastry to cover the filling. Press down around the edges and trim off any excess pastry. Make a small cross in the centre of the pie with a sharp knife to let steam out. Brush with water.

Bake the pie for 15 minutes, then reduce the heat to 190°C/375°F/gas mark 5 and bake for a further 15 minutes, or until golden. Cut into wedges and serve with tomato relish and a garden salad.

Hearty Pastie

It's nearly impossible to buy a decent pastie, so why not make your own? If you don't have the vegies listed here, substitute the equivalent weight of almost anything else you have in the crisper, such as sweetcorn, swede, turnip, mushrooms or cauliflower. Any leftover vegetable mixture makes a fabulous stew.

Serves 2.

2 tablespoons olive oil

2 garlic cloves, finely chopped

1–2 red chillies, seeds removed and finely chopped

1 medium-sized onion

1 medium-sized carrot

1 medium-sized potato

1 medium-sized parsnip

1 medium-sized red capsicum (bell pepper)

100 g (4 oz) pumpkin

1 celery stalk

100 g (1 cup) fresh or frozen peas

200 g (7 oz) silken tofu

2 tablespoons tomato paste

50 g (¼ cup) pinenuts

several sprigs of fresh thyme or oregano or parsley

sea salt and cracked black pepper to taste

1 recipe Rustic Pastry (see page 128) or commercial shortcrust pastry

Preheat the oven to 200°C/400°F/gas mark 6.

Cut all of the vegetables (except the peas!) into small cubes.

Warm the oil in a large heavy-based saucepan over a medium heat and gently fry the garlic and chilli for a minute without browning. Add all the vegies, except the peas, and cook for 10 minutes on a medium heat, until the vegies start to soften, stirring often. Add the peas, tofu, tomato paste, pinenuts and thyme and cook for a further 5 minutes, stirring often.

On a sheet of greaseproof paper, roll the pastry out to just under 1 cm (⅓ in) thickness.

Spoon the vegetable mixture into the centre of the pastry and, lifting the edges of the greaseproof paper, bring the pastry edges to the centre. Press them together so you end up with a seam running along the top of the pastie. Press the sides together with your thumb for a nice imprint. Brush with water. (If you prefer, you could make 2 individual pasties.)

Transfer the pastie, still on the greaseproof paper, to a baking tray. Bake for 10 minutes, then reduce heat to 180°C/350°F/gas mark 4 and bake for a further 30 minutes, until golden. Serve with a green salad and homemade tomato sauce (ketchup) or relish.

Quick idea

Sweet and Sticky Onions

Peel onions and slice. Heat some olive oil in a saucepan and add some finely chopped garlic. Add the onions and stir until evenly coated. Season with salt and pepper. Reduce the heat to low and cook for 1 hour, stirring from time to time. Add some brown sugar and balsamic vinegar to taste and cook until caramelised and sweet.

Vegetarian Shepherd's Pie

Who said the shepherd wasn't vegetarian? You can make this a day ahead and simply warm through to serve.

Serves 4.

1.5 kg (3 lb) potato, sweet potato or pumpkin, peeled and chopped

1 tablespoon olive oil

1 leek, diced

1 garlic clove, finely chopped

1 red chilli, finely chopped, optional

100 g (about ½ cup) dried green lentils, such as Puy

1 medium-sized carrot, diced

1 medium-sized parsnip, diced

2½ cups (21 fl oz) water or Stock (see page 56)

1 x 400 g (14 oz) can crushed tomatoes

1½ tablespoons tomato paste

sea salt and cracked black pepper to taste

50 g (about ½ cup) fresh or frozen peas

50 g (about ½ cup) sweetcorn kernels

1 teaspoon tamari

a small handful of chopped parsley

2 tablespoons sesame seeds

50 g (2 oz) grated parmesan, optional

Preheat oven to 180°C/350°F/gas mark 4.

Peel and cut the potatoes into large chunks. Cover with cold water in a large saucepan and boil over a medium heat for 15 minutes, or until tender. Mash, adding a little water, vegetable stock or oat/rice/soy drink for a smoother consistency. Season to taste with salt and pepper and set aside.

Meanwhile, warm the oil in a large saucepan over a medium heat and gently fry the leek, garlic and chilli for a minute, until the leek softens. Add the lentils, carrot and parsnip and fry gently for a few minutes, until the carrot and parsnip start to soften.

Add the stock, crushed tomatoes and tomato paste and bring to the boil. Reduce the heat to medium-low and simmer for 30 minutes. Add the peas, sweetcorn, and tamari and continue to simmer for 10 minutes, until thick.

Stir in the parsley and transfer the lentil mixture to a large ovenproof dish. Cover with mashed potato, smooth the top and sprinkle with sesame seeds and parmesan. Bake for 15 minutes, or until warmed through and the top is golden.

Quick idea

Cauliflower Cheese

Poach a sliced cauliflower in stock until tender. Drain and put in a shallow heatproof dish in a single layer. Add some thyme, goat's milk cheese and parmesan, and season to taste with salt and pepper. Put the dish under a hot grill until the cheese starts to melt and becomes golden brown, about 5 minutes.

Grilled Polenta & Co

Polenta is so versatile and easy to cook. Seve it immediately, piled high, in place of rice, couscous or mash. Or make it ahead, then grill it and let fly with your imagination.

Serves 4.

1 litre (2 pints) water or stock

200 g (1 cup) instant polenta (cornmeal)

olive oil

Prepare a shallow baking pan (about 28 x 19 cm/11 x 7 ½ in) by lining with greaseproof paper.

Bring the water (or stock) to the boil in a large, deep saucepan over a medium heat. Pour in the polenta in a steady stream, whisking all the time so there are no lumps. Continue stirring with a wooden spoon or whisk for 5 minutes, then reduce the heat to low. Stir constantly to ensure the grains don't stick to the bottom of the saucepan for 15–20 minutes, or until the grains are smooth, creamy and coming away from the sides of the saucepan. Towards the end of cooking, add 1 tablespoon olive oil.

Pour the hot polenta into the prepared pan and smooth the surface. Allow to cool a little, then refrigerate for an hour, or until firm.

Cut the polenta into about 8 rectangles, brush lightly with olive oil and grill or barbecue for 5–6 minutes or until the outside browns and crisps.

Alternatively, fry the polenta pieces in a little oil.

Serving suggestions

Gently warm a few sage leaves, olive oil and drizzle over the polenta.

Fry some chopped mushrooms in a little olive oil or butter. Stir in some seeded mustard and spoon over the polenta.

Roast or grill red capsicums (bell peppers) and remove skin. Cut into strips, drizzle with olive oil and stir in some rinsed and drained capers.

Nestle polenta into a bed of baby spinach leaves, spoon on hot Napoli sauce (see page 84) and top with slices of bocconcini and toasted pinenuts.

Cut 8 figs in half and grill or barbecue for 30 seconds on each side. Serve the figs alongside grilled polenta, topped with rocket and parmesan shavings or crumbled blue cheese.

Polentil Mash

Heat some olive oil in a heavy-based saucepan and add some chopped onions and garlic. Fry until softenened, then add ½ cup yellow lentils and 3½ cups stock and bring to the boil. Reduce the heat and cook for 15 minutes, then add ½ cup instant polenta (cornmeal). Reduce the heat to low and cook for 40 minutes, stirring constantly so the mixture remains smooth. Just before serving, add some grated cheese and parsley, and season to taste with salt and pepper.

Polenta Pizza

Perfect for the 4 o'clock munchies.

About 15 pieces.

3 cups (24 fl oz) water

2 cups (16 fl oz) Stock (see page 56)

250 g (1¼ cups) instant polenta (cornmeal)

25 g (⅓ cup) grated parmesan

50 g (⅓ cup) pitted and chopped kalamata olives

50 g (⅓ cup) chopped semi-dried tomatoes

olive oil

tomato chutney to serve

Line a shallow baking pan (30 x 20 cm/12 x 8 in) with greaseproof paper.

Prepare the polenta as for Grilled Polenta (see pages 134–35), stirring in the parmesan, olives and tomatoes towards the end of cooking.

Pour the polenta into the prepared baking pan and smooth the top. Allow to cool a little, then refrigerate for several hours or overnight.

Cut into squares, triangles, circles or stars with a knife and brush with oil. Barbecue or grill the polenta until the outside is brown and crisp, about 5 minutes. Or bake at 200°C/400°F/gas mark 6 for 20 minutes, or until a crust forms. If you like, turn over and crisp the other side. Serve immediately with tomato chutney.

Macho Nachos

Serves 2.

Frijoles (refried beans)

1 tablespoon vegetable oil

1 medium-sized onion, diced

1 garlic clove, finely chopped

½ teaspoon cumin seeds

400 g (1½ cups) cooked mixed beans or
    1 x 400 g (14 oz) can three-bean mix, drained and rinsed

1 x 400 g (14 oz) can crushed tomatoes

good splash hot pepper sauce

To serve

1 recipe Guacamole (see page 79)

200 g (7 oz) baked corn chips

100 g (1½ cups) grated parmesan

1 cup (8 fl oz) yoghurt

Preheat the oven to 180°C/350°F/gas mark 4.

To make the frijoles, heat the oil in a large heavy-based saucepan over a medium heat and gently fry the onions and garlic and cumin seeds until the onions are soft. Add the beans, tomatoes and a dash of hot pepper sauce and cook for 15 minutes, stirring often, until the mixture thickens.

Meanwhile, prepare the Guacamole following the instructions on page 79.

To assemble, cover a large heatproof plate with half of the corn chips, top with half the bean mix and half the cheese. Repeat with the rest of the ingredients.

Put the plate in the oven for 15–20 minutes, until the cheese is golden. Serve immediately, topped with guacamole and yoghurt. Or serve them separately.

Three-Way Dhal

Served with rice, this always takes me on a passage back to India. It's also good with bread, potatoes or pasta, or if you add vegie stock, you've got a luscious soup.

Serves 2.

100 g (½ cup) yellow split peas

100 g (½ cup) red lentils

50 g (¼ cup) mung beans

1–2 tablespoons ghee, butter or oil

2–3 garlic cloves, finely chopped

1 dried chilli, finely chopped

½ teaspoon black mustard seeds

½ teaspoon ground turmeric

3 cardamom pods, crushed

1 onion, diced

1–2 tablespoons sambar masala

3 cups (24 fl oz) water

sea salt and cracked black pepper to taste

a squeeze of lemon juice

1–2 tablespoons sheep's milk yoghurt

Rinse the peas, lentils and beans well until the water runs clear.

Wam the ghee in a large heavy-based saucepan over a low heat before adding the garlic, chilli mustard seeds, turmeric and cardamom and fry gently for a few minutes, until aromatic. Turn the heat up to medium and toss in the onion, peas, lentils and beans and the sambar masala. Fry gently for a few minutes, until the onion starts to soften.

Add the water and bring it to the boil, then reduce the heat to low, cover, and simmer for 40 minutes. Remove the lid and continue to cook gently for another 20 minutes, stirring often so mixture doesn't burn. If you like a thinner consistency, add more water. Stir in a squeeze of lemon juice and season to taste with salt and pepper.

Just before serving, stir in the yoghurt for a lovely creamy flavour.

Dhal 'solidifies' when cold, so reheat leftovers in the microwave it or warm it over a low heat in a saucepan, adding a little more ghee if necessary.

Quick idea

Braised Fennel

Heat some olive oil in a heavy-based saucepan. Add a thinly sliced fennel bulb and fry gently. Add a cup of stock, bring to the boil, then reduce the heat to low and simmer for 10 minutes. Add some sage and walnuts and season to taste with salt and pepper. Cook until the fennel is tender.

Sounds like me after a training ride on a summer's day, but those three words actually describe some of my favourite meals.

Stirred, Stuffed & Roasted

Tofu and Vegie Stir-fry

When I'm hungry, this is usually the first dish that comes to mind. I cook it often and never tire of it.

Serves 2.

1 small bunch bok choy, stalks removed

1 red capsicum (bell pepper)

100 g (3½ oz) mushrooms

100 g (3½ oz) snowpeas (mange-tout)

1 tablespoon peanut oil

½ onion, sliced lengthwise

2 garlic cloves, finely chopped

1 red chilli, finely chopped (seeds removed, if liked)

300 g (about 10 oz) firm tofu, diced or sliced

2 tablespoons hoisin sauce

1 tablespoon tamari

1 teaspoon sesame oil

2 teaspoons arrowroot or cornflour (cornstarch),
    mixed to a paste with 1 tablespoon cold water (optional)

Cut the base off each bok choy and wash well. If large, cut in half. Remove stem and seeds from capsicum and cut lengthwise into slices. Cut the mushrooms into thick slices, discarding stalks. Top and tail the snow peas, removing strings.

Heat the oil in a wok over a high temperature and add the onion, garlic and chilli. Stir-fry for 1 minute, until aromatic. Add the tofu and stir-fry until golden. Add the vegies and stir-fry for 2 minutes, until they just start to wilt. Mix the hoisin sauce, tamari and sesame oil together in a small bowl, then add to the wok. Stir for 1 minute. (If you prefer a thicker sauce, add the arrowroot and water and stir until the liquid boils.) Serve immediately, perhaps with brown rice.

Roasted Vegetables

You can never cook too many roasted vegies – they taste even better the next day. Make sure all the pieces are roughly the same size so they cook evenly. To hurry things along, microwave or steam the vegetables (except the tomatoes and mushrooms) for a few minutes before roasting.

Serves 2.

2 tablespoons olive oil

2 garlic cloves, finely chopped

2–3 sprigs fresh rosemary

sea salt and cracked black pepper to taste

4 baby carrots, peeled and stems intact

2 small potatoes, peeled

2 parsnip, peeled

1 sweet potato, peeled

2 baby beetroot (beets), well scrubbed and stems intact

1 onion, cut into wedges

2 button mushrooms, peeled but left whole

2 tomatoes, cut in half lengthwise

Preheat oven to 200°C/400°F/gas mark 6. Line 2 baking trays with greaseproof paper.

Place the olive oil, garlic, and rosemary into a large mixing bowl and stir to combine. Put all of the vegies, except the tomatoes and mushrooms, into the bowl and toss to coat. Season to taste with salt and pepper.

Place the vegetables on the baking trays and bake for 40 minutes, turning occasionally to cook evenly.

Put the tomatoes and mushrooms in a bowl and stir gently to coat with oil. Add to the baking tray and bake for a further 15 minutes, until all vegetables are tender.

143

Stuffed Spuds

Writer Shirley Conran reckoned life was too short to stuff a mushroom. Maybe so, but the same can't be said for these vegetables.

Serves 2.

2 large potatoes, skins on

150 g (5 oz) low-fat ricotta or cottage cheese

1 garlic clove, finely chopped

a few fresh thyme leaves

sea salt and cracked black pepper to taste

Preheat the oven to 220°C/425°F/gas mark 7.

Scrub the potatoes well and bake potatoes for 1 hour, or until tender. Carefully cut them in half and scoop the potatoes out without breaking the skin.

In a medium-sized mixing bowl, mash the potato with the remaining ingredients, pile the filling back into the potato skins and serve.

Stuffed Pumpkin

Choose small pumpkins, such as golden nuggets, Minikins or sweet (dumpling) pumpkins.

Serves 2.

2 small pumpkins, skin on

1 cup freshly squeezed orange juice (about 2 oranges)

100 g (3½ oz) chopped dried apricots

100 g (3½ oz) chopped prunes

220 g (1 cup) couscous

25 g (¼ cup) chopped pecans

Preheat the oven to 220°C/425°F/gas mark 7.

Wash the pumpkins well and bake the whole pumpkins for 30 minutes, or until tender.

Meanwhile, heat the orange juice until hot but not boiling. Put the apricots and prunes in a medium-sized mixing bowl. Pour the juice over the dried fruit and steep for 30 minutes.

Add the couscous and pecans to the fruit mixture and stir until well combined.

Carefully slice a lid off the stalk end and scoop out and discard seeds. Scoop out the flesh and combine it with the fruit mixture. Pile the mixture back into the pumpkin shell, Put the 'lid' back on and return the pumpkin to the oven for a further 20–30 minutes, or until tender.

Stuffed Red Capsicum

You can use any coloured capsicum, or a combination, but I like the red ones best. Look for ones with flat bottoms so they won't fall over in the oven.

Serves 2.

2 red capsicum (bell peppers)

1 cup cooked brown rice

1 garlic clove, finely chopped

50 g (1½ oz) goat's milk feta, crumbled

25 g (1 oz) roughly chopped cashews

½–1 teaspoon paprika

1 tablespoon finely chopped parsley

sea salt and cracked black pepper to taste

Preheat the oven to 180°C/350°F/gas mark 4.

Cut lids off the stem ends and remove the seeds and white membranes.

Pack the capsicums into a loaf tin to keep them upright, put the 'lids' back on and bake for 30 minutes.

Meanwhile, combine all the remaining ingredients in a medium-sized mixing bowl. Put the stuffing into the capsicums and return to the oven for a further 15 minutes, or until tender.

Stuffed Zucchini

This has a subtle flavour I just love.

Serves 2.

2 medium-sized zucchini (courgettes)

¼ cup fresh breadcrumbs

50 g (¼ cup) grated parmesan

50 g (¼ cup) shelled and roughly chopped pistachios

4 tablespoons olive oil

sea salt and cracked black pepper to taste

Preheat the oven to 180°C/350°F/gas mark 4.

Cut the zucchini in half lengthwise and scoop out and discard the seeds. Put the zucchini in a small baking dish and bake for 15 minutes.

Meanwhile, combine all the remaining ingredients in a small mixing bowl. Press the stuffing into the zucchini cavity and bake for a further 15 minutes, or until the zucchini is tender and the stuffing is golden brown.

Reggie's Spinach and Feta Filo Parcels

My friend Reggie makes one big parcel for each person, but if you prefer, you can make smaller snack-sized triangles or one large pie. Cover the unused filo sheets with foil or waxed paper and a damp tea towel while you work so it doesn't dry out and become brittle.

Serves 2.

50 g (¼ cup) pinenuts

1 bunch spinach or silverbeet (Swiss chard)

1 tablespoon olive oil

1 onion, finely chopped

4 filo pastry sheets

1 tablespoon olive oil

50 g (2 oz) crumbled feta

freshly grated nutmeg

cracked black pepper

olive oil

Preheat the oven to 190°C/375°F/gas mark 5. Prepare a large baking tray by lining with greaseproof paper.

Toast the pinenuts without oil in a small heavy saucepan. Shake the pan constantly and watch them closely so they don't burn. When just golden, remove from the heat immediately and set aside.

Wash the spinach well. Remove and discard the roots and stalks and roughly chop the leaves.

Warm oil over a medium heat in a large saucepan and gently fry the onion for 2 minutes, or until soft. Add the spinach and cook until it barely wilts. Put the onion and spinach in a large mixing bowl with the pinenuts, feta, a little nutmeg and black pepper, and stir until just combined.

Lay out a sheet of filo pastry and brush with a little olive oil (or water if preferred). Cover with another sheet of filo. Spoon some of the mixture on to the bottom left-hand corner, then fold the bottom right-hand point of the pastry diagonally over filling to the left-hand edge. Seal the edges by brushing lightly with oil and pressing gently. Fold the triangle up over itself and continue folding until all of the pastry is used. Brush with oil. Repeat for the remaining parcel.

Cook for 30 minutes, or until golden brown. Serve hot or cold with a green salad.

• To make snack-sized triangles, cut the filo sheets into 8 cm (3 in) strips and proceed as for large triangles, using 1 tablespoon spinach–feta filling in each. To make a large pie, cut the sheets in half. Lay half the sheets into an oiled metal baking dish, brushing oil between each sheet. Pile in the filling and cover with the remaining sheets, each brushed with oil.

Two four six eight, bog in don't wait. Here are 8 no-fuss recipes for when you are starving and you need food fast.

Fast Food

Asparagus

Break off woody stem and lightly steam for 5 minutes. Refresh under cold water so asparagus stays green (and so you can eat it quicker). Grate some parmesan cheese and crack some pepper over the spears; or add a squeeze some lemon juice; or top with slivered almonds and drizzle with good olive oil and salt and pepper.

Corn on the Cob

Keep the corn wrapped in its own husk. Microwave one cob on HIGH for 2 minutes. Check that it has cooked by peeling back the husk. Alternatively, remove the husk and steam for 5–7 minutes. Season with salt and pepper.

Microwave Sweet Potatoes

Using a fork or skewer, make several holes in the skin. Put potato in a covered container with a small amount of water. Cook on HIGH for 5 minutes, or until tender.

Instant Miso

Bring 2 cups (16 fl oz) water, freshly grated ginger, finely chopped garlic and 1 tablespoon miso paste to the boil and stir until miso is dissolved. Add 25 g (1 oz) dried vermicelli rice noodles, 100 g (4 oz) firm tofu chopped into small cubes and chopped white and green parts of spring onions (scallions). Add one beaten egg. Continue to boil for a few minutes. Season with tamari.

Facing page: Ginger and Lemongrass Risotto (recipe pages 104–5).

Chinese Bread and Butter

Heat 1 cup cooked rice in the microwave for 30 seconds. Add a knob of butter and a dash of tamari.

Boiled Eggs

Cover the eggs with cold water in a small saucepan and bring to the boil – 4 minutes for soft boiled eggs and 8 minutes for hard-boiled eggs. Remember to prick the end to avoid the shell cracking and losing its contents. Soft-boiled eggs can be eaten with toasted bread soldiers, or mashed on to toast and seasoned with salt and pepper.

Egg Toast

Beat one egg with cinnamon, nutmeg and a little brown sugar in a shallow bowl. Soak 2 pieces of bread in the egg mixture. Using a non-stick frying pan, cook the bread on each side until golden brown.

3 Tin Tucker

This is great if the fridge is empty or you are camping. Gently fry a clove of garlic and red chilli (seeds removed) in a small amount of olive oil. Add a 200 g (7 oz) can each of cannellini beans, crushed tomatoes and peas. Season with salt and pepper and a good dash of hot pepper sauce. Add fresh parsley. Bring to the boil and continue to simmer for 5–10 minutes – long enough for everything to warm through. Serve on a thick piece of crusty white toast.

Facing page: Vegetable Ragout (recipe pages 118–19).

Sweet bits are an essential part of every life.
Think moderation, not elimination, and enjoy!

Sweets

Anzac Biscuits

Anzac biscuits are part of Australia's history, becoming popular during World War I, when ingredients such as eggs were scarce. I prefer to make mine with wholemeal flour and raw sugar for a more caramel-flavoured, less processed biscuit.

Makes 15–20.

1 cup rolled oats

1 cup wholemeal flour

1 cup shredded coconut

½ cup raw sugar

25 g (1 oz) butter

3 tablespoons rice syrup or honey or golden syrup

1 teaspoon baking powder (baking soda)

4 tablespoons boiling water

Preheat the oven to 150–160°C/gas mark 2/3. Line a baking tray with greaseproof paper.

In a medium-sized bowl, mix together the oats, flour, coconut and sugar.

In a saucepan, melt the butter and rice syrup over a low heat and stir until well combined. Pour the butter and rice syrup into the rolled oats mixture and stir.

In a cup, mix together the baking soda and boiling water, then add to other ingredients. Stir until everything is well combined.

Form the mixture into balls and place on the baking tray, leaving plenty of room for spreading. Bake for 15–20 minutes, or until golden brown.

Allow to cool a little before transferring to a wire rack to cool completely.

Sparkling Scones

Quick to make, easy to love. Remember to treat the dough gently if you want light scones. And if you don't have sparkling wine, you could always use lemonade or beer.

Makes 24.

4 cups self-raising flour

300 ml (10 fl oz) sparkling wine

1 cup (8 fl oz) reduced-fat cream

Preheat the oven to 210°C/425°F/gas mark 7 and line a baking tray with greaseproof paper.

Sift the flour into a large mixing bowl and make a hollow in the centre. Pour in the sparking wine and cream and mix lightly to make a soft dough. Turn out on to a lightly floured board and knead lightly.

Carefully roll the dough to about 3 cm (1½ in) thick. Cut rounds with a cookie cutter or the rim of a glass. Form a ball with the leftover dough, roll and cut until you have used all the dough. Place the scones on the baking tray and brush the tops with water. Bake for about 15 minutes, or until the tops are golden. Serve warm or cold with strawberry jam.

Loadsa Fruit Cake

'Industrial strength' . . . 'a meal in a slice' . . . 'moist and magic'. These are the comments served up when this cake has been sliced up. For some festive cheer, add a slosh of brandy to the dried fruit.

Makes 1 cake (about 16 servings).

800 g (about 1½ lb) dried fruit, such as sultanas (golden raisins), apple, apricots, prunes and dried cranberries

1 cup (8 fl oz) boiling water

zest of 1 orange

zest of 1 lemon

1 cup (8 fl oz) freshly squeezed orange juice, or orange and lemon juice

¼ cup apricot jam or marmalade

1½ cups unbleached plain (all-purpose) flour

¼ cup wholemeal flour

1 teaspoons baking powder (baking soda)

1 teaspoon cinnamon

1 teaspoon nutmeg

125 g (4 oz) butter, cubed and at room temperature

2 eggs, beaten

extra water, if needed

50 g (1½ oz) whole raw almonds

Chop the larger dried fruit so everything is the same size. Place the dried fruit in a large bowl with the boiling water, orange and lemon zest and juice and apricot. Stirring well to mix. Leave the fruit to soak overnight to become plump.

The next day, preheat the oven to 140°C/290°/gas mark 2. Line a large springform cake tin with greaseproof paper.

Sift the flours, baking soda and spices together into a large mixing bowl. Rub in the butter until the mixture resembles breadcrumbs. Add the beaten eggs and mix well.

Stir in the plumped fruit, ensuring it is well combined and there are no lumps of batter (excellent work for the arm muscles).

Pour the mixture to the lined cake tin, smoothing the surface and making a small indentation in the middle so the top rises evenly. Press the almonds into the top to form a pattern.

Bake for about 2 hours, or until it browns and a skewer inserted in the centre comes out clean. Cover the cake with more greaseproof paper if it is browning too quickly.

Allow the cake to cool in the tin for 15–20 minutes. Turn it out carefully to finish cooling on a wire rack.

Sticky Fruit and Nut Balls

An after-dinner treat or a little something for the lunchbox. Experiment with other types of dried fruit and nuts (except peanuts).

Makes about 12.

100 g (3½ oz) shelled pistachios

50 g (1½ oz) blanched almonds

100 g (3½ oz) dried apricots

3 tablespoons rosewater or water or orange juice or apricot nectar

caster (granulated) sugar

slivered almonds to serve

Put the pistachios, apricots, blanched almonds and rosewater in a food processor and blend until mix well combined. Roll the mixture into balls (about 1 teaspoon, or the size of a small walnut) in your hands. Place on a plate and sprinkle with a little caster sugar. Top each ball with a piece of slivered almond. Eat.

Hairy Date Balls

A perfect afternoon pick-me-up with a cup of tea.

Makes 18.

100 g (3½ oz) pitted dates, roughly chopped

100 g (3½ oz) ricotta

100 g (3½ oz) chopped walnuts

100 g (3½ oz) one-minute oats

½ cup shredded coconut

Put the dates, ricotta and walnuts into a food processor and blend until it mixes well and forms a ball. (Redistribute the mixture around the blades so it combines thoroughly.)

Transfer the mixture to a bowl and stir in the rolled oats. Roll the mixture into small balls and place on a plate. Put the coconut in a saucer and roll each ball in it to coat. Chill before serving.

Chocolate Fruit

The ultimate in yin and yang! It's a simple idea that can be tricked up other ways. Substitute any dried fruits or nuts you like.

Makes 1 punnet strawberries.

200 g (7 oz) good dark chocolate

1 punnet strawberries

dried apple

brazil nuts

Cover a tray with foil or greaseproof paper.

Slowly melt the chocolate in a double saucepan over simmering water.

Dip the fruit and nuts into the chocolate, using a toothpick if necessary, and carefully place on the prepared tray. Chill in the fridge until the chocolate sets.

For a dessert guaranteed to start conversation, dip a whole banana in melted chocolate and roll it in shredded coconut. Chill.

Dissolve 2 teaspoons of instant coffee into the melting chocolate for a mocha taste sensation.

Add ¼ teaspoon chilli powder for another taste dimension!

Indian Honeyed Fruit and Nut Mixture

This is based on an all-purpose salve I encountered in India. It's considered a cure-all, but it doesn't taste like any other medicine I know. A tablespoon will perk up a breakfast dish or dessert or can be eaten as a snack. Substitute any dried fruits or nuts you like. Pistachios, for example, are delicious.

Makes 400 g (14 oz).

100 g (3½ oz) whole dried apricots

100 g (3½ oz) whole dried figs

50 g (1½ oz) sultanas (golden raisins)

50 g (1½ oz) almonds

50 g (1½ oz) cashews

50 g (1½ oz) pepitas (pumpkin seeds)

2 cups organic cold-pressed honey

a few saffron threads

Combine all the fruits and nuts in a bowl and mix well. Transfer the fruit and nuts to a large sterilised jar (3-cup capacity).

Warm the honey gently in a small heavy-based saucepan, but don't let it bubble or boil. Alternatively, microwave for 1 minute. Add the saffron to the honey and stir until well mixed. Allow the honey to stand for a few minutes to allow the saffron to infuse, then pour the honey into the jar over the fruit. Allow to cool, then cover with the lid.

It can be eaten immediately but will keep unrefrigerated for ages, although the fruit and nuts will soften.

163

Berry Tofu Ice-cream

This is terrific for people who can't tolerate dairy, but I eat it because I love it.

Makes about 750 ml (3 cups).

250 g (9 oz) mixed berries

600 g (20 oz) soft or silken tofu

½ cup honey or apple concentrate or rice syrup

passionfruit pulp to serve

Put the berries in a food processor or blender and whiz until smooth. Add the tofu and honey and blend it again until you get a smooth consistency.

Transfer the mixture to a plastic container. Cover tightly with plastic wrap and freeze for a couple of hours, until almost firm. Remove from the freezer and mash or stir to break up the ice crystals. When smooth, refreeze overnight.

Serve with passionfruit pulp. It is also good with a couple of teaspoons of strawberry liqueur and warm chocolate syrup.

Big Kids' Jelly

Why should kids have all the fun?

Makes 1 large serving bowl.

3 teaspoons agar agar

½ cup caster (granulated) sugar

1½ cups (12½ fl oz) boiling water

1½ cups (12½ fl oz) dessert wine

Place the agar agar, sugar and water in a medium-sized saucepan and dissolve over a medium heat for 5 minutes.

Set aside to cool a little, then add the wine and mix well. Pour the mixture into individual glasses or one large serving bowl and refrigerate for several hours, or until set. Serve with fresh fruit and yoghurt.

Banana and Cardamom Puffs

Cardamom has an intoxicating flavour that is so right with banana.

Serves 4.

1 firm, ripe banana

½ cup (4 fl oz) lime juice

1 teaspoon brown sugar

½ teaspoon crushed cardamom pods or ground cardamom

1 sheet frozen puff pastry

1 tablespoon flaked almonds

water

Preheat the oven to 220°C/425°F/gas mark 7. Line a baking tray with greaseproof paper.

Peel the bananas and cut into half lengthwise, then cut each of these across so you have 4 pieces. Place the slices in a small bowl with the lime juice, sugar and cardamom and mix gently to coat well.

Cut the pastry into quarters and place one piece of banana on a piece of pastry with a little of the juice and some of the almonds. Fold the pastry over to wrap the banana and seal by pressing the edges together. Repeat with the remaining pieces of banana and pastry.

Transfer the banana puffs to the prepared tray and brush each with a little water.

Bake for 15–20 minutes, or until golden brown. Serve warm, perhaps with one of the Cream Cheaters (see page 175).

Quick Fruit Tarts

Take a can of your favourite fruit, or a mixture of fruits, and minutes later, dessert is served.

1 sheet frozen puff pastry or 6 sheets filo pastry

1 x 400 g (14 oz) can apricot, peach, pear or apple halves, well drained

water

Preheat the oven to 220°C/425°F/gas mark 7. Line a baking tray with greaseproof paper.

Place the pastry on the bench and arrange the fruit on the pastry sheet, making, for example, four tarts by cutting the pastry into quarters and putting the drained fruit in the centre, with 5 cm (2 in) of pastry all around.

Carefully transfer each tart to the baking tray and brush the pastry with water.

Bake for 15–20 minutes or until the pastry is golden brown. Serve warm.

If using filo pastry, put one sheet down, lightly brush with olive oil, then put another on top. Continue until all the sheets have been used. Continue as above, but do not brush the pastry with water.

Black Rice Pudding

I first encountered this in Bali, where people eat this as an afternoon pick-me-up. But it makes a fantastic dessert with sliced mango or banana, pureed berries or poached tamarillo.

Serves 4.

1 cup black glutinous rice

2 litres (4 pints) water

1 pandan (screwpine) leaf, tied in a knot

2 cinnamon sticks

a pinch of sea salt

400 ml (14 fl oz) low-fat coconut milk

200 g (7 oz) palm sugar (or brown sugar)

½ vanilla bean or 1 teaspoon vanilla extract

Rinse the rice well and soak it 2 cups (16 fl oz) water for 6 hours or overnight.

Put the rice in a large heavy-based saucepan or heatproof casserole dish and add 6 cups (3 pints) water, the pandan leaf, cinnamon sticks, and salt and cook on medium-high for 40 minutes, or until the rice is soft. Stir often and add more water if it dries out.

Stir in the coconut milk, palm sugar and vanilla bean and simmer for 20 minutes, or until palm sugar is dissolved.

For a thicker rice pudding, add only 5 cups (1½ pints) water and cook on low for about 40 minutes.

Facing page: Black Rice Pudding (recipe this page).

Honey-grilled Fruits with Mango Salsa

A spectacular-looking platter for kids of all ages.

Serves 2.

2 slices fresh pineapple

1 banana, cut lengthways and in half

1 peach, cut in half and pitted

1 fig, cut in half

½ cup honey, or as needed

oil for brushing

Mango Salsa

1 mango, cut into small dice

juice of 1 lime

a few roughly chopped mint leaves

1 teaspoon brown sugar (optional)

Heat the grill (oven grill or stovetop griddle), or a barbecue, to high; lightly brush with oil.

Warm the honey gently in a saucepan or the microwave so that it is easy to spread. Brush warm honey over the fruit and grill or barbecue each piece for a few minutes, until golden. Turn and cook the other side.

To make the Mango Salsa, mix the mango with the lime juice and mint together in a small bowl.

Arrange the cooked fruit on a platter or individual plates, spoon on a little of the mango salsa and serve warm.

Facing page: Loadsa Fruit Cake (recipe pages 158–59).

Apricots Baked with Orange and Ginger

A lovely breakfast dish or dessert eaten hot or cold. Try it sometime with a combination of dried fruits instead of just apricots.

Serves 2 generously.

200 g (7 oz) dried apricots

1 cup (8 fl oz) freshly squeezed orange juice (about 4 oranges)

zest of 1 orange

1 cup (8 fl oz) water

2 cm (¾ in) piece fresh ginger, grated

4 chopped mint leaves to serve

yoghurt (optional)

Preheat the oven to 180°C/350°F/gas mark 4.

Place the apricots, orange juice and zest, water and ginger in a large baking dish (about 18 x 26 x 5 cm/7 x 10 x 2 in).

Cover the dish with a lid or foil and bake for an hour, until the apricots have absorbed most of the liquid.

Serve warm or cold, sprinkled with chopped mint and yoghurt, if desired.

To make a rich dessert, replace some (or all) of the water with brandy, sherry or a sticky wine. Dollop on mascarpone cheese.

Baked Stuffed Apples

Winter just isn't the same without this old fave.

Serves 2.

2 firm Granny Smith or Red Delicious or Royal Gala apples

50 g (1½ oz) finely chopped pecans

50 g (1½ oz) chopped dried pears or any other dried fruit

50 g (1½ oz) sultanas (golden raisins)

zest of ½ orange

a sprinkling of ground cinnamon

a sprinkling of ground cloves

¼ cup honey

yoghurt to serve

Preheat the oven to 200°C/400°F/gas mark 6.

Gently pierce the apple skins with a fork or skewer. Remove the cores and a little of the surrounding flesh with a corer or sharp paring knife.

Combine the pecans, pears, sultanas, orange zest, cinnamon and cloves in a small bowl. Stir until well combined.

Spoon the mixture into centres of each and gently push down. Place apples on a baking tray and cook for 45–50 minutes, or until tender. Test by inserting a skewer: if there is little resistance, the apples are ready.

Warm the honey (about a two minutes in a saucepan or 10–20 seconds in the microwave) and drizzle it over the apples. Serve with a dollop of yoghurt.

Baked Blueberry Tofu Cheesecake

Compared with traditional cheesecakes, this is low in fat. But it's every bit as good.

Makes 1 (about 6 servings).

150 g (5 oz) rolled oats

50 g (1½ oz) butter

½ cup (4 fl oz) water

400 g (14 oz) firm tofu

½ cup brown sugar

½ cup (4 fl oz) lemon juice (about 2 lemons)

1 teaspoon vanilla extract

200 g (7 oz) blueberries

Topping

2 tablespoons brown sugar

50 g (1½ oz) shredded coconut

50 g (1½ oz) pecans, roughly chopped

1 teaspoon ground cinnamon

Preheat the oven to 180°C/350°F/gas mark 4.

Mix the rolled oats in a food processor for a minute until crumbly then pour into a large mixing bowl.

Melt the butter and pour over the rolled oats. Mix well, then add the water and stir again.

Press the mixture into the base of a springform cake tin to make a firm crust.

Blend the tofu, sugar, lemon juice and vanilla essence to a smooth paste. Stir in the whole berries, then pour the mixture over the crust and bake for 30 minutes, or until set. Remove the cheesecake from the oven and turn it up to 200°C/400°F/gas mark 6.

Combine the topping ingredients and sprinkle on to cheesecake. Bake for a further 5 minutes. Remove from the oven and allow to cool slightly before removing from the tin. Serve warm or cold, perhaps with poached fruit.

Bread and Banana Pudding

This takes me back to my childhood, only then, the pudding was loaded with butter and cream. Here is a lower-fat version that's just as delicious. Use fresh white bread, soy and linseed bread or a thinly sliced dense fruit loaf.

Serves 4.

2 bananas, sliced lengthwise and in half

100 g (½ cup) sultanas (golden raisins)

8–16 slices bread (depending on size), crusts removed

2 cups (16 fl oz) rice/oat/soy drink

2 eggs, beaten

1 tablespoon brown sugar

1 teaspoon ground cinnamon

1 teaspoon ground nutmeg

1 teaspoon vanilla extract

Preheat the oven to 180°C/350°F/gas mark 4.

Lightly grease a large, deep baking dish (about 28 x 22 x 6 cm/11 x 9 x 3 in) or 4 individual ramekins. Place the bread on the base and add the banana. Sprinkle sultanas over the banana and cover with bread.

Beat the milk, eggs, sugar, cinnamon, nutmeg and vanilla essence in a medium-sized mixing bowl until well mixed. Pour over the bread and bananas.

Press the bread gently and let it stand for 10 minutes. Bake for 45 minutes (less for ramekins), or until the centre is set.

Cream Cheaters

Sweet little somethings to serve alongside dessert for those times when you feel like going wild but don't want the calories or fat content of full cream.

Ricotta Cream

200 g (7 oz) smooth low-fat ricotta

50 g (¼ cup) pistachio nuts, chopped roughly

2 teaspoons ground cinnamon

Put the ingredients in a small bowl and mix well to combine.

Vanilla Cream

200 g (7 oz) yoghurt

½ vanilla bean, cut in half again and seeds removed or 1 teaspoon vanilla extract

50 g (1½ oz) pecans, chopped

1 tablespoon honey

Put the ingredients in a small bowl and mix well to combine.

Nutty Cream

100 g (3½ oz) cashews

1 Granny Smith apple, peeled and cored

1 tablespoon apple concentrate

1 tablespoon yoghurt

1 teaspoon nutmeg

Blend all ingredients until smooth.

Fruity Polenta Crumble

Moreish is the only word to describe this wheat-free crumble.

Serves 4–6.

100 g (1 cup) rolled oats

200 g (1 cup) polenta

100 g (4 oz) butter, melted

½ cup brown sugar

½ cup water

500 g (1 lb) apples or pears, peeled, cored and diced

1 bunch rhubarb, washed, leaves discarded and cut in 4 cm (1½ in) lengths

100 g (3½ oz) sultanas (golden raisins)

a sprinkling of ground cinnamon

a sprinkling of ground nutmeg

zest and juice of 1 lemon

yoghurt to serve

Preheat oven to 180°C/350°F/gas mark 4.

Combine the oats, polenta, melted butter, sugar and water in a bowl and mix well.

Place the diced apple in a saucepan and just cover with water. Simmer for 10 minutes. Add the rhubarb and simmer for a further 5 minutes.

Remove from the heat, add the sultanas, lemon zest and juice, cinnamon and nutmeg and stir until well combined.

Transfer the mixture to a deep ovenproof dish. Cover with the crumble mixture and bake for 15–20 minutes, or until the crumble topping is golden. Serve hot, with yoghurt.

Toffee Shards

Oooh, posh! They'll think you've been slaving for hours when you stick a shard of toffee into a ball of ice-cream or scatter small pieces over poached or stewed fruit. But take care: toffee burns are horrible.

Makes 1 baking sheet's worth.

3 cups caster (granulated) sugar

1 cup (8 fl oz) water

½ cup (4 fl oz) brown vinegar

1 cup (8 fl oz) boiling water

crushed nuts (almonds, pecans, and sesame seeds), shredded coconut or hundreds and thousands

Line a baking tray with greaseproof paper. Set aside.

Place the sugar, cold water and vinegar into a medium-sized heavy-based saucepan. Stir over a low heat until the sugar dissolves. Using a pastry brush dipped in the boiling water, brush the sides of the saucepan to remove any sugar that has splashed up the sides.

Bring to the boil on a hight temperature without stirring and boil for 15 minutes, or until a small amount dropped into cold water 'cracks' (stiffens and breaks).

When the toffee is cooked, remove the saucepan from the heat and stand it in cold water for 1 minute, until all the bubbles subside.

Very carefully pour the toffee mixture into the baking tray to form a thin layer. Let it stand for a few minutes, then sprinkle on nuts, seeds or hundreds and thousands.

Allow the toffee to cool completely before carefully breaking into shards.

• If you want the toffee to be more like a crumble, put into a plastic bag and bash with a rolling pin.

Conversions

Solid Measures

30 g	1 oz
50 g	1½ oz
100 g	3 oz
125 g	4 oz
150 g	5 oz
180 g	6 oz
200 g	7 oz
250 g	9 oz
500 g	1 lb
1 kg	2 lb

Liquid Measures

1 metric teaspoon	5 ml
1 metric tablespoon	20 ml
1 US tablespoon	15 ml
¼ metric cup	60 ml (2 fl oz)
½ metric cup	125 ml (4 fl oz)
1 metric cup	250 ml (8 fl oz)
4 metric cups	1 litre (2 pints)

Some Equivalents

1 cup almond meal	110 g (3½ oz)
1 cup cornflour (cornstarch)	100 g (3½ oz)
1 cup raw couscous	180 g (6 oz)
1 cup flour (plain and self-raising)	125 g (4 oz)
1 cup raw lentils	220 g (7 oz)
1 cup rolled oats	100 g (3½ oz)
1 cup peas	170 g (5½ oz)
1 cup polenta (cornmeal)	180 g (6 oz)
1 cup raw rice	220 g (7 oz)
1 cup sugar, brown	200 g (7 oz)
1 cup sugar, caster (granulated)	225 g (7 oz)
1 cup sugar, icing (confectioners')	125 g (4 oz)

Glossary

ALMOND MEAL   Ground almonds. You can buy them in a packet or process whole raw almonds at home.

ALOE VERA LIQUID   Aloe vera has been described as a natural healer as it contains many essential amino acids, vitamins, minerals, proteins and enzymes.

AMARANTH   A tiny grain that hails from the Incas and a good source of protein. Purchase from health-food stores and supermarkets.

APPLE BUTTER/PURÉE   Apple butter is a thick sauce readily available at supermarkets but you can make it at home by cooking down apples until they form a thick purée. It contains no butter, and is lovely in sandwiches, on roast vegetables and in some cakes.

APPLE JELLY   A wobbly spread with the same use as apple butter/purée.

APPLE/PEAR CONCENTRATE   A thick liquid made from concentrated apple or pear juice, used as a sugar substitute.

ARAME   A mild, sweet-flavoured seaweed. Packets of dried arame are available from Asian grocers and health foodstores. To use, cover arame with water in a small saucepan over a medium heat, bring to the boil and continue to boil for 5 minutes. Drain.

ARROWROOT   A cornflour substitute that is useful for those who suffer Coeliac's disease. Used as a thickener for soups and stews.

BANANA CHIPS   Fried or baked bananas, great for adding to muesli or as a snack.

BARLEY FLAKES   They look like rolled oats and are made by rolling pearl barley. Great for porridge or used in muffins and cakes.

BIRD'S EYE CHILLI   A small red chilli, usually used in Thai and other South-east Asian curries. Very hot, so try as you go.

BLACK BEAN SAUCE   Can be bought readymade from Asian foodstores. A thick, dark and rich sauce made from black beans and soybeans, fabulous for stews, casseroles and stirfries.

BOCCONCINI   A fresh cheese similar to mozzarella, available fresh from delicatessens. They come as white balls of varying sizes.

BUFFALO MOZZARELLA   A sweet mozzarella made from buffalo milk. If you can't find it, use bocconcini.

CELERIAC   Related to celery, celeriac is a bulbous root. To use, peel and slice. It tastes stronger than celery, but one can easily be substituted for the other.

CHICKPEAS   Has a high content of vitamin B15 and fibre. Chickpeas and other beans are suitable for diabetics because they help to lower blood sugar levels.

CHILLI JAM   A sweet and spicy sauce available at Asian foodstores. Use on stir-fries and roast veggies. I use it like tomato sauce.

CHINESE PICKLED GINGER   Thinly sliced ginger in vinegar with a light pinkish blush, sold in jars in Asian stores.

COUSCOUS   A tiny yellow grain that is very versatile and can be eaten for breakfast, lunch and dinner. It is produced from wheat and is high in carbohydrates.

CRACKED WHEAT   Also burghul, bulgur or bourghal. Hulled, parboiled, dried and ground wheat grains.

CRAISINS   Dried cranberries. Can be found in packets in supermarkets.

DIJONNAISE   A blend of seeded mustard and mayonnaise.

DRIED FRIED SHALLOTS   Deep-fried sliced shallots, available in packets or jars from Asian foodstores. Use as a garnish on soups or stir-fries.

DRIED SHIITAKE MUSHROOMS   Also called dried Chinese mushrooms, these add an earthy, smoky flavour to stir-fries and soups. To use, soak the mushrooms in some warm water until the caps are soft. Remove and discard the stem and slice the caps before using.

EDAMAME   Soybeans in their pods, available frozen from some Asian grocers and health foodstores. Edamame have almost equal amounts of protein and carbohydrates with only a little fat.

ENOKI MUSHROOMS   You can buy these fresh or canned at most supermarkets or Asian foodstores.

FREEKAH   Young green wheat that can be cooked and used like rice.

FRIED BEAN CAKE   Available from Asian foodstores and some supermarkets, it is similar to deep-fried tofu.

GALANGAL   A member of the ginger family, and looks like a cross between ginger and turmeric. The pinkish root is mostly used in Asian-style cookery.

GHEE   Clarified butter, mostly used in Indian cookery.

GREEN TEA NOODLES   Soba (buckwheat noodles) with powdered green tea added to the noodle dough.

HOISIN SAUCE   A dark, sweet and spicy sauce. Good as a marinade, or splash in a stir-fry.

HON SHIMEJI MUSHROOMS   Fresh Japanese-style mushrooms, available from most supermarkets or Asian stores.

KAFFIR LIME LEAVES   Fragrant leaves that are notable for their double leaf. Fresh is best, but they freeze well. Available from greengrocers and good supermarkets.

KELP GRANULES   Seaweed granules, available in boxes at supermarkets.

KOHLRABI   A bulbous-looking white or purple vegetable that has a slightly peppery taste.

KOMBU OR KONBU   Dried kelp, usually sold in 13–15 cm/5–6 in dried black strips covered with a fine white powder that adds a delicate, salty-sweet sea flavour to food. It contains essential amino acids, vitamins and minerals, plus glutamic acid, which flavours and softens beans, making them easier to digest. Sold in health foodstores and Japanese grocers.

LECITHIN   Soft granules with similar properties to eggs, available in packets from health foodstores and some supermarkets.

LEMONGRASS   Long firm stems with a lemony smell and flavour.

LSA   Ground linseed, sesame seeds and almonds, available ready-blended from supermarkets and health foodstores. Or buy the individual components and make your own.

MINIKIN, SWEET PUMPKIN OR GOLDEN NUGGET PUMPKINS   Small varieties of pumpkin.

MIRIN   Japanese sweet rice wine, used in cooking.

MISO PASTE   Fermented soybean paste, indispensable in Japanese soups.

MOUNTAIN BREAD   Flat bread that has no yeast.

NORI SHEETS   Thin sheets of dried seaweed, available in packets from Japanese grocers. Used in sushi.

OAT MILK   Milk made from oats, good for people who are lactose intolerant.

OKRA   A green vegetable that looks like little green fingers, used in soups and stews.

ORANGE BLOSSOM WATER   The essence of orange flowers, sold in bottles in health foodstores and delicatessens. You only need a few drops for a lovely aroma and flavour.

OYSTER MUSHROOMS   Large, flat, pale mushrooms you can buy fresh at most supermarkets or Asian stores.

PANDAN LEAVES   These add a lovely vanilla-like fragrance and flavour to Asian sweets and desserts. Tie the leaves in a knot to make them easier to pull out of the dish. Available from Asian grocers, often frozen.

PITA BREAD   A thin unleavened bread that can be split to be filled.

POLENTA   Also called cornmeal, this is dried, ground corn (maize). It is high in fibre, low in fat and a great source of carbohydrate, ideal for those who cannot tolerate gluten.

POWDERED WHEATGRASS   For those times when you can't get fresh wheatgrass. Available from health food shops.

PSYLLIUM HUSKS   The ground husk of psyllium seeds. Can be sprinkled on cereal or muesli and added to bread and muffins for extra fibre.

QUINOA   Pronounced keen-wa, this ancient grain is available at health foodstores and some supermarkets. It is a good source of carbohydrate, magnesium, iron and potassium. It also contains more protein than most cereals and grains.

RICE FLAKES Flakes made from rice, ideal for use in cereal.

RICE FLOUR A great substitute for those who cannot tolerate gluten.

RICE MILK Milk made from rice. For those who cannot tolerate lactose.

RICEPAPER WRAPPERS Thin dried sheets made from a rice flour batter, used in Vietnamese cooking. Wet the wrappers before use.

RICE SYRUP Looks like honey and runs like honey but is made from rice and can be used as a sugar substitute. Vegans use it as a honey substitute.

RICE VERMICELLI NOODLES Thin clear noodles made from rice. Soak in hot water until soft, then use in ricepaper rolls and noodle soup.

RISONI Pasta shaped like rice grains, used in soups.

ROGAN (ROGHAN) JOSH PASTE An Indian curry paste blend. There are many commercial varieties with varying degrees of heat.

ROSEWATER Distilled from rose petals, this clear liquid is sold in health foodstores and delicatessens, and adds a lovely sweet flavour and smell to drinks or food.

RYE FLAKES Flakes made from rye grain, used in breakfast cereals.

SAMBAR MASALA A spice paste, available from any Indian speciality store.

SEMI-DRIED TOMATOES Partially dried tomatoes, available from good delicatessens and supermarkets.

SEMOLINA The heart of the wheat kernel, used in porridge, puddings, soups and pasta.

SESAME SEEDS To toast, place the seeds in a medium-hot saucepan or under the griller and allow to cook for a few minutes. Watch that they don't go brown.

SHAO HSING WINE Also called Chinese cooking wine or Chinese rice wine. If you can't find it, use dry sherry or mirin.

SHIITAKE MUSHROOMS See dried shiitake mushrooms.

SHOYU Japanese-style organic soy sauce.

SILKEN TOFU The softest of all types of tofu, available in the refrigerator section of Asian foodstores and supermarkets.

SOBA Japanese-style buckwheat noodles.

SORJ An unleavened flatbread.

SORREL A salad leaf with quite a tart taste. Use rocket or mustard leaves if you can't find sorrel.

SPICED TOFU Available from Asian foodstores and some supermarkets.

TAHINI Sesame paste, used as a butter substitute or in hummus or as a salad dressing.

TAMARI Thick Japanese soy sauce.

TANGELO A citrus that is a cross between a mandarin and grapefruit.

TEMPEH Tempeh is usually made from fermented soybeans with different varieties made from wheat, rice, millet and peanuts. It's very versatile and is great in casseroles and stews but can be baked, fried, marinated, steamed.

TOFU PUFFS Little puffy squares of tofu, available from Asian foodstores and some supermarkets.

TRITICALE A hybrid grain created by crossing wheat with rye. Available from supermarkets or health foodstores.

WASABI A bright green paste, indispensable in Japanese sushi, that is similar in taste to horseradish and mustard.

WHEAT GERM Fine flakes from the germ of wheat, which is rich in vitamins, minerals and protein.

WILD RICE Not a rice but the seed of a barley-like North American aquatic grass. It has a nutty flavour and a chewy texture.

Index